MW00529555

THE ANTHROPOLOGY
OF UTOPIA

For Ruth & John,
with love,
Dan Chodorkoff
10-28-14

THE ANTHROPOLOGY OF UTOPIA

DAN CHODORKOFF

ON SOCIAL ECOLOGY AND COMMUNITY DEVELOPMENT

ESSAYS

new-compass.net

The Anthropology of Utopia:
Essays on Social Ecology and Community Development
2014 © Dan Chodorkoff

ISBN 978-82-93064-30-5
ISBN 978-82-93064-31-2 (ebook)

Published by New Compass Press
Grenmarsvegen 12
N–3912 Porsgrunn
Norway

Design and layout by Eirik Eiglad

New Compass presents ideas on participatory democracy, social ecology, and movement building—for a free, secular, and ecological society.

New Compass is Camilla Svendsen Skriung, Sveinung Legard, Eirik Eiglad, Peter Munsterman, Kristian Widqvist, Lisa Roth, Camilla Hansen, Jakob Zethelius.

new-compass.net
2014

CONTENTS

Editorial note: These essays were written over a period of several decades, but have all been considerably edited for this publication. "Social Ecology and Community Development" was first published in John P. Clark (editor), *Renewing the Earth: The Promise of Social Ecology* (London: Green Print, 1990). "Redefining Development" appeared in *Society and Nature: International Journal of Political Ecology*, 7 (1995). "Toward a Reconstructive Anthropology" is a previously unpublished manuscript; it was written in 1982 and has been used extensively by students at the Institute for Social Ecology. "Alternative Technology and Urban Reconstruction" is also previously unpublished: in 2010 it was submitted to *Communalism: A Social Ecology Journal* (the precursor of New Compass Press), and was the essay that prompted us to turn this into a book project. "The Utopian Impulse" was originally published in *Harbinger: The Journal of Social Ecology*, 1 (1983). "Social Ecology: An Ecological Humanism" is a previously unpublished manuscript, while "Education for Social Change" originated in a lecture Chodorkoff gave in New York City to the Friends of the Modern School, in September 1998. "Occupy Your Neighborhood" was published at the ISE blog in October 2012. Chodorkoff's "Introduction" was written in 2014, specifically for this book. Eirik Eiglad, Jakob Zethelius, and Peter Munsterman prepared this collection of essays for publication.

INTRODUCTION

We face an unprecedented crisis of global dimensions. Our reliance on fossil fuels and chemical substances that poison our earth, water, and atmosphere requires more than dramatic shifts in policy; it requires that we begin to conceptualize and actualize new institutions and relationships that can move us away from these destructive practices. How can we reharmonize people and nature? How can we create an ecological society?

These fundamental questions animate these essays. I believe that social ecology offers a set of ideas that may help us formulate a comprehensive response to the crisis we are facing. It suggests not only a transformation of the underlying political and economic structures of our society, but, equally important, the creation of a new sensibility that reflects a qualitatively different understanding of peoples relationship to nature and, indeed, a redefinition of nature itself. Such a far-ranging transformation directly challenges our current global systems of hierarchy, domination, and exploitation. Social ecology believes that the creation of these new institutions and relationships is both possible and necessary.

A grandiose project? Perhaps. But my background as an anthropologist has shown me that much of what we assume to be the natural order of things are, in fact, products of our particular culture; of a historical trajectory which reinforces and then reifies our current institutions and relationships based on greed, competition, aggression, and domination as expressions of "human nature." In developing a new praxis we must go beyond such a narrow, culture-bound concept of "human nature," and look for a broader understanding of "human potential," a continuum that, while it undeniably encompasses greed, competition, aggression, and domination, also contains the possibilities of care, cooperation, nurturance, and unity in diversity. This collection of essays suggests that our current assumptions about our "nature" are an expression of only one set of the wide range of possibilities open to us as a species.

Such a call for radical change may seem naïve, and I must begin with a confession, I have spent much of my life, both personal and professional, pursuing utopia. Not the cloud cuckoo land of fabulists, nor the dream world of religion, rather I have tried to seek the far shores of real possibilities: a just, ecological society. My involvement in a wide range of popular movements, coupled with my personal journey through collectives, co-ops, and squats, led me to the academic study of literary, historical, and philosophical utopias. By being both a participant and observer within utopian social movements, I have tried to grasp what I call "the anthropology of utopia." Admittedly, it is often a study of shadows and flickers, of short-lived "festivals of the oppressed" and movements stopped far short of their goals. But it is also the study of potentiality actualized, of gardens growing in ghettos, and direct democratic community assemblies.

I spent forty of those years working with the Institute for Social Ecology (ISE), which I co-founded with Murray Bookchin in 1974. We envisioned an institute for radical education, forwarding the ideas of a decentralized and democratic, ecological revolution. The institute was intended to be radical in form, in content, and in intent: a place where we could educate people about the skills and ideas that can help to create an ecological society.

The ISE has always emphasized the unity of theory and practice. In the early years we focused on technical studies in then-pioneering areas like wind power, solar energy, organic agriculture, and aquaculture, which we understood as critical for the decentralization of food and energy production. Such a self-reliant material base was seen as a precondition for community control and direct democracy allowing for the creation of a confederation of self-managed eco-communities. However, we understood that such techniques and technologies were necessary, but in and of themselves not sufficient to bring an ecological society into being. We emphasized the need to develop a conscious, ethical approach to social organization, based in the understanding that all environmental problems are really social problems, and that our attempts to dominate nature grow out of the domination of humans by other humans.

These concerns led us to offer classes in philosophies of nature; to explore the anthropology of cultures that could give us insight into qualitatively different forms of social organization and attitudes toward nature; and to study a range of revolutionary and utopian traditions. Our concern with *praxis*— theory and practice continually informing each other and interacting in a developmental dynamic—was carried into the realm of social action through involvement in community development efforts and ecological movements. We worked with ideas related to organizational forms, tactics, and long-range strategies: many of these ideas have since become common practice in contemporary social movements and in community development projects.

I was privileged to participate in the development and application of those ideas in my as executive director of the ISE, where we saw our mission, in part, as educating educators and organizers; helping to spread the ideas to an ever-widening group of people. We did that through formal, credit-bearing and degree-granting programs, and through various forms of popular education: conferences, workshops, lectures, internships, and hands-on experiences in organic gardening, renewable energy, and ecological design, as well as in community organizing and political activism.

Here in the United States, the ISE has been involved in many of the radical environmental movements of the last 40 years, ranging from the movement for alternative technology and popular struggles around both nuclear weapons and nuclear power, where we worked with the Clamshell and Shad Alliances, to the emergence of the eco-feminist movement, the formation of the Green movement, the movement against genetically modified organisms, the anti-globalization movement, the climate justice movement, and most recently, the occupy movement. We also worked on community development projects with the Puerto Rican community on New York's Lower East Side, Ramapo Mountain People in New Jersey, rural Vermonters, and Tzotsil speaking Maya people in Chiapas, Mexico. We also published journals, newsletters, pamphlets and books related to social ecology. These outreach efforts have contributed to the creation of an informal international network of social ecologists in the Americas, Europe, Australia, Asia, and Africa. In the essays that follow I reflect on some of those experiences.

This anthology opens with the essay "Social Ecology and Community Development," which discusses the ways in which economic development is often conflated with the development of community. Community development, however, is a much more complex and nuanced process, one which ultimately rests on the creation or recreation of affective ties among people, and their participation in generating a common vision for the future of their community. Grassroots planning, political action, arts and culture, all play important roles in how we can physically transform our neighborhoods and build community. This piece is in large part inspired by my twelve years of involvement in grassroots community development efforts in Loisaida, the Hispanic section of New York City's Lower East Side.

Development is a theme that carries over into the next essay, "Redefining Development," which offers a critique of international development efforts like those promoted by the World Bank and the International Monetary Fund. This essay was written at a time when structural adjustment programs were imposed on developing nations by international funders—with devastating effects. Over a 30-year period of travel and study in Chiapas, Mexico, I observed first hand the destructive cultural and ecological impact of the large-scale internationally funded development projects, with little or no benefit accruing to the indigenous Mayan people of the region. In the current era, while the players have largely shifted from the international agencies discussed in this essay to private sector investors, the dynamics have largely remained the same; calling for lower taxes, privatization, and deregulation in the name of "free trade." Further, we have seen these same policies promulgated in the developed world under the rubric of austerity. I suggest that these approaches are essentially anti-ecological and colonial in nature.

All of these essays are written from the perspective of anthropology, the discipline I chose to study and the lens through which I approach social ecology. I was drawn to anthropology because it seemed to me one of the few academic disciplines that allowed one to explore the breadth of the human experience. Anthropology is essentially integrative in its efforts to understand human development and its central concept—culture—is at its core holistic. At the same time, I am deeply ambivalent toward my chosen profession: I recognize its tainted origins in colonialism as well as its methodological and practical limitations. In "Toward a Reconstructive Anthropology" I offer a critique of academic anthropology and suggest a reformulation of the discipline; I believe this might help anthropologists to overcome those limitations and actively engage with its important insights. Anthropology has much to offer the world, but it must move out of the classrooms and into our communities if its full potential is to be realized.

I return to the community development process in Loisaida in "Alternative Technology and Urban Reconstruction," where I examine aspects of that work in greater depth. I focus on the experience of CHARAS, a community group that introduced alternative technologies and organic food production to their urban neighborhood. In doing so they developed new forms of leadership and a directly democratic approach to community planning that, for a time, successfully contested the city's plans for the transformation of their neighborhood.

To create a truly ecological society I believe we need to transcend the given and imagine something that, while rooted in real, existing potentialities, is qualitatively different from what exists today. In "The Utopian Impulse" I sort through a variety of aspects of utopian thought and action that have emerged in history, and I present a typology of utopias; I also explicate the importance of the utopian mode of thought as a form of social analysis that directs us toward the future. Today, given the depths of the crises we face, utopian thinking is more important than ever. I do not suggest that utopia should be interpreted as a "blueprint" for a new society, but rather as a set of principles; with the understanding that the details will have to be worked out by individual communities.

These essays all revolve around the ideas of social ecology, which is a complex, interdisciplinary perspective that draws on studies in philosophy, anthropology, history, biology, and ecology. Social ecology presents a framework for analyzing people's relationship to nature, and advocates a reconstructive perspective to reharmonize people and the rest of nature. It cannot be reduced to a bumper sticker or be defined in 25 words or less, it is an approach ill suited to the age of Twitter. Yet it also deserves an explication that does not require a PhD in critical theory to understand. This is what I try to provide in "Social Ecology: An Ecological Humanism," which gives a brief outline of the main components of social ecology, encompassing its basic philosophical concepts, its anthropological perspective, its interdisciplinary character, and some of its political implications.

Education, too, is an essential part of any great social change, and I have spent most of my life as an educator, but never in a traditional setting. There are many different forms that education can take, the classroom being one important arena, but not the exclusive terrain for meaningful learning. "Education for Social Change" offers a critique of traditional education and its "hidden curriculum," and explores the pedagogy that has animated the ISE. I profoundly believe that we need to "learn our way" out of our current morass together.

The final essay in this collection, "Occupy Your Neighborhood," is of more recent origin. Social movements ebb and flow over the course of years and I have been lucky enough to be there at the high ebb of several significant movements. I arrived at Zucotti Park on the second day of the occupation and was astounded to see Wall Street awash in a "festival of the oppressed." Like many long in the tooth radicals I was inspired by both the message and the method of the Occupy Wall Street movement. ISE alumnae and faculty were among the initiators, and we were privileged to offer several weeklong seminars to key organizers. The meteoric rise and then the decline of Occupy in popular culture led me to reflect on its strengths and prospects as well as its weaknesses and limitations, and, most importantly, on the potentiality of new developments like Occupy Sandy to help us find a way out of the conundrum of protest politics.

We are limited in part by our imaginations. The hegemony of the dominant paradigm has blinded us and bound us to a world of buying and selling. But human potentiality is what gives me hope: our very ability to transcend the given and turn what is into what could be. I have been chasing this dream of another world for 50 years. This may be a futile pursuit, but over those years I have seen many of the ideas that grew out of these utopian experiments take root in the popular imagination, and, in the words of Errico Malatesta, "Everything depends on what people are capable of wanting."

I offer these essays in a spirit of humility. They are not scholarly essays, but personal reflections and analyses. As a cultural anthropologist, and in recent years as a novelist, I am, by training and inclination, a storyteller. I have tried to make the ideas presented here accessible, and interpreted my experience in light of these ideas. These essays contain no answers: the solutions to the problems we face must arise from the communities to which the reader belongs. But my hope is that this collection of essays contains insights that resonate with readers and, most importantly, suggests to them ways in which they might apply these ideas in their own context, to help bring an ecological society into being.

SOCIAL ECOLOGY AND COMMUNITY DEVELOPMENT

Social ecology, as developed by Murray Bookchin, brilliantly presents a comprehensive theoretical framework for analyzing the crises of modernity. It is perhaps the first such comprehensive approach since Marx, and suggests a reconstructive practice which holds promise of fundamentally transforming people's relation to nature and to other people. The ultimate promise of social ecology is the reharmonization of culture and nature. A vital element in that profound transformation lies in the connection between social ecology and community development.

Community development is an often-abused concept. Perhaps the best way to begin to define it is to state what it is not. As I use the term, community development is not the delivery of services to a needy population by professionals. This is the traditional model put forward for decades by professional development agencies. It is the War on Poverty model that views communities as battlefields on which "strategic resources" must be brought to bear. It calls for bureaucratic intervention on a massive scale to improve education, health care, housing, nutrition, economic opportunity, and other facets of a community's life. Needless to say, these goals must be incorporated into any meaningful approach to community development. The problem lies with the methodology, the process whereby these noble ends are achieved.

A Holistic Approach to Community Development

True community development cannot rest on a foundation of outsiders delivering services. Such an approach inevitably fosters dependence on external "experts" and "resources." This dependency hinders the development of indigenous leadership, broad participation and local self-reliance. Ultimately, it often degenerates into a form of social control, strengthening subordination to the dominant culture, furthering the homogenization of communities, and reinforcing centralization of power and policymaking in the hands of outsiders. This approach leads to the disempowerment of communities and citizens, not their development.

Nor can we understand community development in the terms conservatives have presented it since the Reagan administration. Their position is reactionary to the core, and lacks even the good intentions of the War on Poverty approach. They suggest a policy rooted in private-sector investment and a "trickle down" effect that can lead only to exploitation, domination and community disintegration. Here too, the focus is on absorbing communities into the mainstream of the dominant culture.

The linchpin of this strategy is to offer incentives for private enterprise to "develop" a community, thus subsidizing its subjugation. Domestic "enterprise zones" have been proposed which would replicate the domination of Third World nations by corporate investments. The intention is to offer a package of tax deferments, relaxed health and safety standards, and an elimination of both anti-pollution measures and the minimum wage, in order to entice private industry to invest in economically depressed communities.

The definition of community development here is economic. The assumption is that business will provide jobs, jobs equal income, and increased income constitutes community development. Yet, the reality is that although such an approach may possibly increase income for individual community members, it is done at the cost of cultural tradition, community cohesion, a healthy physical environment, and community control of important resources.

A more benign form of private-sector development was attempted in the early 1970s under the rubric of "Black Capitalism." Here the effort targeted individual entrepreneurs within a community and aided them in their efforts to establish small businesses. A similar expectation of prosperity "trickling down" underlay this approach. The reality of Black

Capitalism was that the majority of these enterprises failed, unable to compete with their more highly capitalized, better organized corporate competition, and the few that succeeded brought prosperity only to their owners and to a handful of employees. As a result, they increased social stratification in the communities they were supposed to develop.

Another traditional approach to community development, "urban renewal" through city planning, has had an equally dismal record. The failure of ambitious plans for the rehabilitation of massive areas has been well documented. Yet, planners persist in imposing new spatial relations on neighborhoods with the expectation that their designs can create community. While architecture and planning can help to reinforce particular social relations, community development is not a "design" problem. Grandiose plans for urban renewal reflect a technocratic mentality that permeates our civilization, a belief in the quick fix of technics. Historically, people have understood that design requires integration into the social life of a community if it is to enhance the quality of life. Sure enough, there exists a tradition that recognizes the holistic nature of community design, but the technocrats who populate professional planning largely ignore it.

The tendency of our society to seek technical fixes, technological solutions to what are essentially social problems, is a strong one, and has been carried over into community development efforts. The introduction of "alternative technologies" into the community development schemes of the 1970s constitutes a case in point. Alternative technology was given a central role in a variety of pilot projects for community development during the Carter administration. But the model of introduction was, in too many cases, one of experts setting up technical systems without significant community participation. As a result, certain ghetto neighborhoods are now littered with rusting solar collectors, nonfunctional windmills, and graffiti-covered greenhouses. The "technological solution" to community development means no solution at all.

In addition to the institutionalized approaches that have been described over the past two decades, there have also been a variety of efforts at grassroots community development, some of which have met with more success. These efforts have largely focused on the issues of community participation and control of local institutions like school boards, planning boards, and specific programs in housing and job training. Many of their concerns and approaches to change parallel those of social ecology.

True community development, from the perspective of social ecology, must be a holistic process that integrates all facets of a community's life. Social, political, economic, artistic, ethical, and spiritual dimensions must all be seen as part of a whole. They must be made to work together and to reinforce one another. For this reason, the development process must proceed from a self-conscious understanding of their interrelationships.

The dominant culture has fragmented and isolated social life into distinct realms of experience. The rediscovery of the organic ties between these realms is the starting point for the development process. Once they are recognized, it is possible to create holistic approaches to development that reintegrate all the elements of a community into a cohesive dynamic of cultural change. Here, social ecology draws an important principle from both nature and "primitive" society: the integrative character of life in both natural ecosystems and organic communities.

A Critical Analysis of Everyday Life

The everyday life of a community needs to be critically analyzed. Which relationships work, and which are nonfunctional? Are there traditions of mutualism and cooperation existent that can help a community to realize its goals, or must new forms be created? How can the face-to-face primary ties that characterized pre-bureaucratic societies be recreated in the context of contemporary community?

Is there an existing political sphere that can be expanded and transformed to empower the community? Town meetings, block associations, neighborhood planning assemblies, and popular referenda are all vehicles that can be revitalized through the process of community development. How do the existing governmental structures stand in relation to the community development process? The reclamation of politics by the community and the creation of an active citizenry are, from the perspective of social ecology, critical elements in community development.

How can the arts aid in community? Poetry, music, community murals, ritual drama, and literature can all help to foster a unique identity and to reinforce a community's sensibility, if fully integrated into the process.

The spiritual element of a community is important in the developmental matrix as well. From where does a community derive its values, its ethics, and the principles that orient its development? What is its cosmology? How can it gain the inspiration needed to sustain it through the long, difficult process of cultural reconstruction?

The social realm, including family structure, women's roles, social networks like clubs, gangs, and cliques must be examined as well. These relationships underlie many of a community's formal elements, and provide the clearest connection to the primary ties that need to be recreated.

The integration of relational ties, the cultural traditions, myths, folklore, spiritual beliefs, cosmology, ritual forms, political associations, technical skills, and knowledge of a community is crucial. All of these elements must be brought together to provide a base for development. These extra-economic factors are the critical components almost always ignored by the traditional development approaches. But the concern of social ecology is with the development of *community*, not mere economics. Economic development not rooted in a comprehensive understanding of community may well have a disintegrative effect.

However, the economics of a community, and here I use the term in the broadest sense, as its productive relations, are a vitally important aspect of the project. Who owns and controls the productive resources in a community? What can it do to develop its material base, particularly in the crucial areas of food and energy production? How can technology be used in the process? Are there existing functional or vestigial cooperative economic forms or traditions that can be utilized? Food co-ops, producers' co-ops, land trusts, common lands, and credit unions offer possibilities in this area.

Recreating Communities

In looking for models of ecological social organization, social ecology recognizes that we must consciously look to history to understand our own potential. For example, it proposes that we can separate the liberatory principles of primitive societies from their superstition, xenophobia, and ignorance. Human development and cultural evolution are not linear processes. We still carry the potential for coherent community within us. It is naive to assume that all was good in the primitive world. However, primitivity as a comparative model allows us to understand all that civilization has lost, and that our cooperative potential as a species is much greater than civilization would have us believe.

The form and sensibility of a community are both shaped by and help to shape its environment. This is equally true of tribal communities, the cities of Mesopotamia and Mesoamerica, the Greek *poleis*, the cities of Renaissance Europe and modern metropolises. In the case of the modern metropolis, however, the true substance of this relationship is clouded by the mediating effects of modern technology and the striving for "mastery" of the natural world. A sense of scale, an organic relationship to a specific environment, have all been central to the authentic sensibility which has informed community life for millennia, a sensibility which has begun to break down only in the very recent past.

This is not to deny the existence of imperial cultures in the past, but to recognize that these existed as a mode of domination, as an overlay of oppression that exacted tribute from the local community. These local communities continued to provide a coherent framework for the social life of their residents, a sense of grounding and support that lay hidden beneath the veneer of empire.

It is the breakdown of local community and its total subjugation to the culture of domination which is unique to our own time. Therefore, a primary task in the process of community development is the recreation of local community, and a key component in that task is the identification of humanly scaled boundaries and the reclamation of a sense of place, be it rural village, small town, or urban neighborhood.

The creation of sensibility of a community—the self-identification of people with place, a sense of commonality, cooperation, and a shared history and destiny—is difficult to achieve, particularly in a social milieu which emphasizes individualism, competition, mobility, and pluralism. The growth of values like individuality rooted in community, cooperation, identification with place, and cultural identity are antithetical to the thrust of the dominant culture. But just as the imperial cultures of the past constituted a mode of domination rather than an authentic form of consociation, the dominant culture of our own time is merely a system of control through exploitation and manipulation. The forms that exploitation and manipulation take have been effective in destroying community, but they have not replaced it. They have left a vacuum, a hollow place in which resonates the neurotic individualism of Western societies and the collective hopelessness of the East. It is that vacuum, with the often unconscious yearning for reconnection it produces, that the community development process must fill.

Social ecology does not propose an abstract ideal society, but rather an evolving process of change, never to be fully realized. For as soon as we approach the ideal, the ideal changes. Engaging reality with the will to transform it opens up a new realm of possibilities. This is the most profound tradition of utopian thinking, a continuation of that of nineteenth century utopian Socialists like Robert Owen and Charles Fourier. Although their plans incorporated fanciful elements, their concern was with a built environment that reinforces community, with an integration of agriculture, industry, social discourse, poetry, spirit, and even, in Fourier's case, emotional diversity. The tradition finds still more explicit expression in the work of the Russian anarchist Peter Kropotkin. To this tradition, social ecology adds a consciously ecological perspective.

The utopian element in the community development process should not be misconstrued. Social ecology understands the limitations of utopia as blueprint, the tendency to retreat from the problems of reality into the cloud cuckoo land of abstract design. It also recognizes the power of utopia as inspiration and as a point of orientation in the day-to-day, incremental process of changing the world. It is the utopian process—holistic, participatory and integrative—that must inform the practice of community development.

Toward Decentralization

This utopian view relies on community empowerment, the ability of a community to consciously plan for its future and to implement those plans. Empowerment can occur only through the creation of real forums for planning and policy-making, forums that are decentralized, participatory, and democratic. Communities must reclaim the public sphere, which has become bureaucratized and professionalized. Old forms may be utilizable or new forms may have to be created, but without the initiative of an active citizenry no forum can serve as a vehicle for community empowerment. Empowerment must be rooted in the full participation of the citizenry in the decision-making process, the reintegration of politics into everyday life.

Social ecology also proclaims the ideal of local self-reliance, and dependence on indigenous resources and talents to the greatest extent possible. This does not, however, mean "self-sufficiency," a condition in which no community has existed since the Neolithic. Self-reliance recognizes and encourages interdependence among communities, but emphasizes an ecologically sustainable ethos in the realms of production and consumption, decentralization in the political sphere, and a healthy respect for diversity.

Confederations must be created to help coordinate cooperative activities between self-reliant communities, to administer those interdependent functions which are recognized, and to work to equalize resources between communities. Social ecology suggests that such confederations might form a "commune of communes," a commonwealth which could extend from the local to the regional to the continental level and beyond, to result in an ultimate unity through diversity. In this goal, social ecology echoes the telos of natural evolution itself: a movement towards ever-greater complexity and diversity within interrelated webs of life.

The tools and techniques needed to develop communities as unique cultural entities based in the concepts of ecological sustainability and local self-reliance are already available. Decentralized, community scaled technologies for energy production can help to support the kind of holistic community development envisioned by social ecology. Solar energy, wind power, and small-scale hydroelectric all offer the potential for renewable, nonpolluting sources of energy. Food-production techniques like French intensive gardening, hydroponics, bioshelter technology, aquaculture and permaculture can provide a good percentage of a community's food needs on a year-round basis. All of these techniques are proven, and many are commercially available. Given a humanly scaled community, the integration of agriculture and industry relying on alternative technologies and advanced, ecologically sound food-production techniques could provide a viable material base for a self-reliant community.

One measure of a community's sustainability and self-reliance lies in the relationship between town and country. Where the city has become totally alienated from the countryside as in contemporary urban society, an unhealthy relationship exists. On the one hand, the city dominates the countryside, draining it of resources for its own use; on the other hand, the city is heavily dependent on the countryside, parasitically requiring energy-subsidized forms of agriculture and transportation for its existence.

The ethos of the dominant culture has fostered a specialization of function, which has excluded food production from most communities. The industrialization of agriculture has created a dangerous centralized approach to food production, in which population centers are dependent on food producers thousands of miles away for their daily sustenance. This is a situation highly vulnerable to a variety of crises, such as crop infestation, energy shortages, and disruptions in transportation. If any of these disruptions occurred, disaster would ensue. This form of food production also has destructive ecological implications, like destruction of soils, loss of genetic diversity, and vulnerability to infestation by fungi and insects.

Historically, healthy communities have achieved a balance between town and country. The Greek *polis* of Athens, for example, consisted of a central city and an outlying agricultural district. The medieval commune integrated gardens within its walls. Even in our own era, there has been a more balanced relationship. New York City, until the 1950s, got much of its food from Long Island and New Jersey. There were dairy farms on Staten Island, and chicken farms in Brooklyn. Today, the regional agricultural economy has broken down.

The relationship between town and country has other, nonmaterial aspects as well. The predominantly rural values of coherent communities have given way, for the most part, to the *anomie* and alienation characteristic of the city. The breakdown of community grows out of this basic shift in values. The Folk-Urban Continuum of Robert Redfield, Ferdinand Tönnies's contrast between *Gemeinschaft* and *Gesellschaft*, and the split noted by Marx between town and country are all paradigms which express a social division that is reflected in our own time by the almost total alienation of community from its basis in nature.

The development of healthy communities requires a rebalancing of town and country, a reintroduction of the organic world into the largely synthetic environment of the city. Such an action may initially be rooted in the purely material realm, as in the introduction, through community initiatives, of green spaces, neighborhood gardens, food parks, permacultures, and the like. This transformation of the physical environment and the introduction of the skills of nurturance and husbandry needed to transform the physical environment will contribute to the development of a new sense of community, which will reflect these skills as social values.

The Holistic Approach in Practice

At this point, a concrete example of community development should help to illustrate the praxis of social ecology. Loisaida is the Puerto Rican section of New York's Lower East Side where residents attempted to actualize elements of this approach in the mid 1970s. There is much to be learned from this experience. Let me describe the way that one of the community's problems was turned into a community resource through the development process.

In Loisaida, there were over one hundred vacant lots. They were rubble-strewn dump heaps, breeding grounds for rats and cockroaches, an eyesore and health hazard. These lots often served as a dangerous "playground" for neighborhood children, and constituted a blight on the community. Viewed from the perspective of social ecology, however, these lots represented a precious community resource: open space. In an environment of concrete and decaying tenements, these lots, a substantial percentage of the land of the neighborhood, offered valuable sites for recreation, education, economic development, and community cultural activity.

Local activists recognized this potential and began the development process at the grass roots, organizing residents to clean up the lots and put them to constructive use. Most of the lots belonged to the city of New York, which had done nothing to improve them. The people of Loisaida combined a critical analysis of their problem with direct action. They protested to the city, and they cleaned the lots themselves and began to use them.

They converted some to "vest-pocket parks," a concept introduced by Robert Nichols, outfitting them with benches and planting green spaces. Others were turned into playgrounds, utilizing recycled material for equipment. Swings were made from discarded lumber and old tires, jungle gyms were built from recycled beams. Other lots were turned into community gardens, which became a focal point for intergenerational contact. One large lot was transformed into an outdoor cultural center, La Plaza Cultural, where community poets, theater groups, and local musicians all performed. Several lots were adopted by local schools for use as teaching centers where area youths were introduced to lessons in agriculture and ecology. The transformation of the lots helped to reintroduce the natural world into this ghetto community.

These were simple actions, but their results were profound. The lots were initially transformed by people acting on their felt need to reconstruct their environment. They acted without the official sanction of the city; in fact, in some cases, it was in the face of opposition from the city. This direct action was a first step towards community empowerment.

The initiative came from within the community, from an indigenous leadership that analyzed the problem and sought a utopian and reconstructive solution. They did not look to the city for a solution; they created their own. They contested with the city for the material base of their community, the land; and, in most cases, they gained either legal leases to the lots for token amounts of money, or outright title. Several community land trusts were created to remove particular lots from the real estate market forever, and to guarantee their continued use as a community resource. A philosophy of "doing more with less," the motto of CHARAS, one of the community groups involved, served as an inspiration to the open-space movement in Loisaida.

Owing to a holistic approach, a number of other elements in the community development process grew out of these simple actions. A problem turned into a resource, and the health of the community benefited as a result. The people involved in the work gained a sense of pride and accomplishment. Several youth gangs were involved in the movement, and their experience in constructive social action helped to bring them off the street. A cooperative was formed to manufacture playground equipment from recycled items, creating jobs and income for the people involved.

The gardening groups drew on the traditions of the Jíbaro, the Puerto Rican peasantry from which many of the Loisaida's residents hail, and thus provide a connection to a living cultural tradition. They were able to draw on a cross-section of the community, young and old, which often remains alienated from the development process. The gardens grew fresh, healthy, organic produce, improving nutrition and lowering food costs for community gardeners. They enhanced the community's self-reliance in an important symbolic way, and the training in gardening led to plans for increasing it further, through the construction of commercial rooftop greenhouses.

The establishment of the cultural plaza created an outdoor space for the celebration of Loisaida's New York Puerto Rican culture. This helped to strengthen the identity of people often traumatized by their move to the mean streets of New York. This identity was central to the development of an effective movement for change in Loisaida.

Perhaps the most significant aspect of the open-space movement was the empowerment of the people involved. The transformation of their vacant lots drew them into a larger vision of what their community might be. The participants in the open-space joined together with other community activists working on issues like health care, education, housing, and job development. Quarterly town meetings were held to chart the progress of the movement, to coordinate and integrate their actions, and to develop a comprehensive plan for the future of the community. An alternative grassroots planning group, the Joint Planning Council, emerged to challenge the official city plan for the Loisaida community, previously a disenfranchised, demoralized ghetto, became a force to be reckoned with in New York, and emerged as a model for grassroots, ecologically oriented approaches to community development.

The incorporation of the ideas of social ecology into the process of community development provided a clear demonstration of the power of Bookchin's theories to further movements for cultural change. Social ecology represents a vital source of ideas that will increasingly find expression in an effective praxis. We must continue to develop and articulate its theories in a holistic framework, because social ecology, by virtue of its comprehensive vision and its truly radical nature, represents a challenge to the basic assumptions of our civilization. It is only by developing such a challenge that we can hope to move through our current crises toward an ecological, harmonious, and peaceful world.

REDEFINING DEVELOPMENT

As the global expansion of "free trade" proceeds at an exponential rate and the ideological hegemony of capital seems assured, it would appear to be a futile exercise to undertake a critical analysis of the basic assumptions of "development." Yet without such a fundamental critique, there is no way to make sense out of the paradox presented by a grow-or-die economic model in an age of diminishing resources and ominously declining environmental quality. In fact, the ecological crises, which we face both in our local communities and on a global scale, can only be understood as an outgrowth of industrial capitalism and traditional models of development. And further, those crises must be seen as social crises, arising from society and our attitudes toward and relationships with each other, not from nonhuman nature. Thus any authentic solution to the "development puzzle" must address both the problematic of the industrial capitalist model and the society of which it is an outgrowth.

Contemporary models of development assume an integration of "undeveloped" nations and communities into the global market, and through that process a rise in economic prosperity and a gradual diminution of the differences in living standards between North and South. Such a transformation requires a massive infusion of capital for infrastructural improvements, usually in the form of international loans, and large-scale investments by multinational corporations to extract resources and create industry and jobs. The results of this approach to development have often been catastrophic, leaving developing areas wallowing in debt, poverty, cultural disintegration—caused by the displacement of local cultures and economic systems—and, finally, ecological devastation.

Rather than creating a stable middle class which can join the ranks of benumbed consumers flourishing in the First World, this approach to development commonly leads to a dual economy consisting of a tiny group of the very rich and a great mass of the very poor. This trend has been well documented in relation to Africa, Asia and Latin America by authors as diverse as Ted Trainer, Lloyd Timberlake, Vandana Shiva, and Rigoberta Menchú. While there has been a dramatic increase in the overall "wealth" of the planet, an ever greater concentration of that wealth is in the hands of fewer and fewer people.

An analysis from the perspective of social ecology suggests that current development models must be firmly rejected if we are ever to achieve an ecological society. In fact, a basic redefinition of "development" is a precondition for the survival of the planet. How then does social ecology define development? How does that definition differ in basic ways from the traditional approach? And what are the means that can bring a new definition to bear in the world? In answering these questions, we must address certain issues in order to redefine development. My treatment of these issues here are intended to be suggestive rather than schematic, and they will need to be applied in different ways in various parts of the world. But they must be, according to Murray Bookchin, the seminal thinker in social ecology, unabashedly utopian in the most profound sense. Utopian thinking today requires no apology. Rarely in history has it been so crucial to draw on the imagination in order to create radical new alternatives to virtually every aspect of daily life.

Quality Versus Quantity

A basic assumption of traditional development models is that bigger is better. Large-scale, centralized projects that require massive infusions of capital consume the vast majority of money spent, and success is usually measured by quantitative means (increases in the Gross National Product, output per worker, per capita income, and so on). Quantitative criteria can reveal trends on a national level, but they do not necessarily tell us anything about the impact of these forms of development on the lives of people. Without a thorough understanding of the social context in which such statistics are being generated, it is actually possible to misinterpret what development means to people's lives. Despite impressive percentage increases in the Gross National Product throughout the developing world, in his 1989 book, *Developed to Death*, Ted Trainer remarks that "the poorest 520 million in these countries are probably seeing their income rise on average about 73 cents per annum."

Even in the industrialized North such figures can be misleading. For example, since the late 1970s the United States has seen a steady increase in the Gross National Product, dramatic gains in worker productivity, and a small increase in per capita income, but the real wages paid to workers have declined, and the number of people living in poverty has increased. However, in a system increasingly dominated by a bottom-line mentality which delegitimizes and degrades anything that stands in the way of profit, such are the costs of progress.

A social ecological perspective on development views the process in terms of quality, not quantity. It requires that we ask an entirely different set of questions. Traditional indices do not provide a framework adequate for the analysis of qualitative impacts. Here I am referring not only to the impact of development on the environment, which some "sustainable" development models do quantify, but more importantly the impact on the quality of life—such as connections and relationships between people, family and kinship bonds, sense of community, maintenance of cultural cohesion, and other criteria that are difficult to measure.

These are critical areas that need to be assessed. It is the development of a higher quality of life—with the economic component as merely one aspect—that must be the overall measure of success.

Quality of life is difficult to quantify. But the goal of development must be focused on providing people with the security that their basic needs, like adequate food and shelter, will be met, as well as what are often intangible areas that are reflected in a sensibility. Well-being undoubtedly requires a degree of economic security, but it rests more on a sense of socio-cultural security. A coherent community and an equitable distribution of even meager resources can often provide more for an individual's economic, social and spiritual needs than an increased income. This point is well illustrated by the success of Kerala, the poorest state in India, which has, through a process of development which rests on redistribution of internal resources during the 1990s, managed to attain India's highest rates of literacy (70 percent versus 36 percent for all of India), and to guarantee access to basic nutrition, health care and education for all of its citizens. The culture of industrial capitalism, while it pays lip service to these values, in fact is the major force undermining them around the globe.

The modern concept of development was born at the Bretton Woods Economic Summit following World War II and led to the establishment of the International Monetary Fund (IMF) and the World Bank. These institutions were designed to finance the rebuilding of Europe after the war. They were operating in a milieu in which the basic assumptions of capitalism were a given. That this model has since been promulgated as a universal path for development speaks to both a basic misunderstanding of the nature of Third and Fourth World cultures, and the arrogance of the West. It is interesting to note that, despite more than 50 years of this type of development, poverty, famine, environmental disaster and the gulf between the rich and poor have been increasing at an almost exponential rate. These facts suggest that there is something basically wrong with the concepts that underlie this model.

Those qualitative aspects of life, upon which any viable form of development must be based, should contain within them an important economic aspect; however, the qualitative must not be subsumed by the economic. In fact, just the opposite is true. If authentic development is to occur, economics must be brought back under the control of society, as it has been for most of humanity's tenure on the planet. The perspective of economic anthropology, most notably the work of Karl Polanyi, supports this view. The social ecology of Murray Bookchin posits this process as the creation of a moral economy. Moral economy sees economic activity not only as a way to provide people with the material means of life, but also as a way of creating affective ties between people and their community.

Much of what passes for development today has the opposite effect. Modernization undermines community and forces people into the market, where they lose their identity as unique individuals and are reduced to a faceless proletariat. The well-documented results of the "Green Revolution" in agriculture present a stunning example of this highly problematic process. A moral economy is perhaps the only alternative to this destructive dynamic. It is the preservation, creation or reinforcement of community and an active citizenry upon which development must focus. These in turn are the preconditions for resolving our ecological crises. Empowerment of people is the real goal of any authentic process of development. Social ecology calls for the primacy of these socio-cultural criteria over the economic. Indeed, it is a revolutionary outlook: it understands the elimination of all relationships based on hierarchy and domination as an integral part of the development process, and as the starting point for a reharmonization of people's relationship with the rest of nature. This perspective challenges in basic ways the institutions of the State and transnational corporations that are the primary vehicles for development under the current model.

Any approach which fails to offer this basic critique, even "alternative" models like "sustainable" development, "trade not aid," or "green" and "caring" capitalism, can only lead to further immiseration, poverty, exploitation, cultural devastation, and ecological destruction. There is a growing literature touting such approaches and a substantial critique developing as well. The criticism of these approaches offered by Survival International reveals their self-serving nature, as well as their underlying logic, which never questions the primacy of the market. The fact is that traditional models of development, far from being the solution to these ills, are in large part the problem. Unless the a priori assumptions of statistic and corporate frameworks are rejected, capitalism will continue to colonize and subvert the cultural and ecological diversity necessary for a healthy planet.

In *Staying Alive*, Vandana Shiva notes that "development as capital accumulation and the commercialization of the economy for the generation of surplus and profits thus involved the reproduction not merely of the particular form of the creation of wealth, but also the associated creation of poverty and dispossession." We need to reorient our thinking about development and find real alternatives. Attempts to create a "caring capitalism" are oxymoronic. The very nature of the global market undermines what should be the goals of development: the promotion of unity in diversity through processes that ensure local communities' economic security, cultural survival and ecological health. Attempts to posit capitalism and the market as appropriate vehicles to bring about these conditions range from the extremely naive to the extraordinarily cynical; for example, the focus of "sustainable" development, as it emerges on the world stage, is finding a means to sustain the expansion of capitalism.

When the Brundtland Commission of the United Nations, in its report *Our Common Future* discusses "sustainable development," it is exactly this process to which it refers. It is the economic realm that currently determines the conditions under which development occurs. Local and particular needs are subsumed under a "global" perspective which views the world as a series of interchangeable parts categorized under the rubric of raw materials, pools of labor, and potential markets. The homogenization of difference is posited as a progressive process. The universalization of the culture of capitalism (such as it is) is viewed as an inevitable and highly desirable outcome. Coca-Cola Redux!

Modernization and Diversity

The problem of modernization is subsumed under a western, linear notion of progress which is rooted in a crude, Social Darwinist view of human history that first surfaced in the nineteenth-century canon of cultural evolution. These ideas were first presented by Herbert Spencer and further elaborated by Frederic William Maitland and Henry Maine and, in the United States, by Lewis Henry Morgan. These schematic views proposed to rank all human cultures in a hierarchy, with Civilization (Western European) at the top and all other forms below. Typically, the hierarchy proceeds from Savagery to Barbarism to Civilization, to use Morgan's nomenclature. Here it is worth noting that Morgan's scheme, as developed in *Ancient Society*, was the basis for Marx and Engels' thinking on this issue, which is one reason that "Marxist" approaches to development have been as destructive as those of capitalism.

The assumption underlying this thinking is that the rest of the world has failed to reach the same level of prosperity as the North because of inherent cultural flaws. They are beneath us because their cultures are inferior to our own. Thus it becomes "the white man's burden" to bring the poor savages and barbarians the benefits of civilization. In the nineteenth century, this line of thinking provided a moralistic rationale for the worst excesses of colonialism and imperialism, and it remains an a priori of traditional approaches to development.

This is not to suggest that Third and Fourth World people do not want access to aspects of modern technology and knowledge, rather that they are offered no choice in the matter. And further, that those elements of modernity that could have a positive impact on their quality of life are often presented only as part and parcel of a thoroughgoing "modernization" which undermines their traditional culture and transforms people into monadic producers and consumers operating as part of the global market. Just as surely as the political domination of the nineteenth century led to oppression, death and destruction, so too does the new colonialism of the IMF, the World Bank and the multinational corporations.

If anything, the neo-colonialism of the global marketeers is more pernicious. In the nineteenth century, empire was a mode of oppression which constituted a thin overlay of exploitative relationships intended to extract raw materials and labor from peoples who were still embedded in their unique cultures. In the late twentieth century we saw the level of exploitation penetrate not only peoples' social and economic relations but their very consciousness as well. Today a diverse world of unique cultures is being denatured and reduced to a collection of interchangeable individual workers and consumers-isolated, exploited and manipulated. Modernization is equated with homogenization—no surprises—in a standardized world producing standardized products for increasingly standardized consumers who confuse freedom with the choice between white and pink toilet paper.

Authentic approaches to development must, from the perspective of social ecology, emphasize a unique developmental path that critically explores the potentialities of every individual culture as a distinct entity. This is not a call for an extreme relativism that uncritically takes every culture on its own terms. Rather it is a recognition of the complexity and diversity inherent in social systems and an examination of each in relation to a set of criteria which are extracted from our interpretation of certain tendencies within natural evolution that enhance ever greater complexity and diversity.

These tendencies include unity in diversity, non-hierarchical relationships, mutualism, spontaneity and co–evolution. These are key principles for us to consider as integral to a process of development that can help to create an ecological society. Every community must have a primary voice in its own development. Decisions regarding the adaptation of elements of modernity must grow out of an extremely self-conscious process, one which weighs not only immediate benefits and risks, but also the long-term cultural implications of every decision. The ecological principles mentioned above help to create an ethical framework, and must be a necessary component of any authentic approach to development. It is the realm of ethics that will allow for a transcendence of the cost accounting methods prevalent among most international development agencies. As Ted Trainer puts it in *Developed to Death*, it calls for a "moral path to development."

The hegemonic position of the culture of capitalism undermines most efforts at maintaining a self-conscious and selective stance vis-à-vis modernization. It is presented as a "take it or leave it" proposition. If a nation questions the prescription of an IMF-style restructuring of economic and development policy, sources of credit and capital will be cut off. With the collapse of Communism and an end to the counter force once represented by the Soviet Union, even the limited options once available to underdeveloped nations have been constricted. The leverage which growing international debt has given to the World Bank and the IMF has effectively shut down the possibility for any creative approaches to development. While individual communities may choose to pursue alternative development models, the nation-states of the developing world must pay homage to the mastery of the market and dance to the tune of international capital.

However, it is the inherent tension between the market forces that power modernization and the ecological imperative to preserve the biological integrity of the planet that holds the potential for a creative resolution. In places where capitalism's assault on the environment is still in its early stages, people have the opportunity to critically analyze the experience of the developed world, to learn from our legacy of ecological devastation and to choose consciously not to replicate our mistakes. The crucial dynamic here is one in which people are able to develop the self-awareness necessary for such an approach to succeed. Increasingly, the pressure to open up markets and bring them into the global economy has taken on an almost religious fervor. The global market has become the holy grail of our time, and to resist the crusade on its behalf is to risk the fate of all unbelievers: dismemberment or death. Yet to not resist inevitably leads to the same end.

Process Versus Product

Traditional development models are geared toward increasing production, greatly enhancing the wealth of those who are in charge of production, and theoretically allowing the crumbs to "trickle down" to the lower level. If, for production to be increased, people have to sacrifice their freedom, their health or the environment, such sacrifice is justified if it results in increased production and a rising Gross National Product.

Social ecology views development as process oriented rather than product obsessed, focused not on production, but on reproduction, on the biological processes that renew the earth. The process of development must be transformed so that it leads to growing empowerment of disempowered sectors of the society, and an increased level of self-consciousness regarding their ability to reorient the direction of development. Development itself must be redefined as the empowerment of communities to determine their own future in an open way, free of the coercion of the IMF, the World Bank and other international development agencies.

As André Gunder Frank pointed out in the sixties, capitalist development fosters dependency on the dominant culture of the rich nations. As long as they define the terms under which development occurs (or does not occur), the chances for a process-oriented form of development, which could allow Third World nations to break out of dependency, are slim indeed.

Current development practice focuses primarily on resource extraction, on creating and exploiting low-cost pools of non-unionized labor, and on agricultural production of crops to be exported to the more affluent nations. In other words the product-oriented approach to development is geared almost exclusively toward production for consumption by the wealthy nations and the tiny ruling elites of the Third World. Ironically, nations like Mexico and Guatemala, which are both large exporters of agricultural products, still have substantial populations suffering from malnutrition and hunger. A growing consciousness of this fact has resulted in popular insurgencies in both countries. The Zapatista rebellion in Mexico focused on the destructive effects of the North American Free Trade Agreement (NAFTA) as a major issue.

The increased globalization of production and the free market ideology of NAFTA and the General Agreement on Tariffs and Trade (GATT) can only further the immiseration of the poor.

Grass roots localized approaches to development, like those proposed by social ecology, would focus first on food security for the people living within the developing nation. Development must be a process of education as much as infrastructure building. It stimulates an unfolding of the productive possibilities in every locality in accord with the specific conditions in that particular place; it is an organic process in which people define their own future, rather than allowing the market to define it for them.

It is an internal process that flows out of communities rather than a process which is externally imposed on them. Much current development in the South is debt driven. International agencies use the leverage that grows out of massive foreign debt to restructure the social policies and political priorities of debtor nations to reflect the needs of international capitalism. The "Shock Therapy" of IMF Structural Adjustment Programs has devastated nation after nation in the South. Often associated with right-wing regimes, these programs have been effective in forcing even "progressive" administrations to redefine their priorities.

A social ecological approach to development begins the process at the grass roots, working with communities at the local level on projects which they have determined will improve their quality of life. Regional and national development priorities then grow out of the local orientation. This dynamic is facilitated by a process of confederation in which each locality has its concerns represented regionally and nationally to allow for the creation of a coordinated strategy for development that is built from the bottom up and reflects the desires of the mass of the population rather than those of the elite.

Perhaps the most radical departure of a social ecological approach to development is its rejection of the market as a viable mechanism for stimulating or facilitating development. In fact, the market stands in direct opposition to the goals of true development. The market demands adherence to a model with built-in winners and losers; it creates dependence on external sources of financing, technology and expertise; it disempowers the local in favor of the impersonal economic forces; it views nature as a "resource" ripe for exploitation; it presupposes a universal standard of affluence modeled on the North which, if ever achieved—and indeed it seems to be an impossibility from an ecological perspective—would result in a homogenization of the world's cultures and ecosystems. We must recognize that dramatic changes in patterns of production and consumption in the North are a precondition for true development in the South.

The assimilation of the diverse cultures of the planet is the human parallel to the loss of biodiversity that our current development practice foreshadows. It is only through active resistance to the dominant model and the creation of real alternatives which exist outside of the framework of the global market that there is hope for the authentic development of the peoples of the planet, an unfolding of potentialities that could allow us to achieve the more profound ground of a humanity which is both rooted in the varied lives of the world's diverse peoples and cultures and truly universal in its ethical stance and practice.

TOWARD A RECONSTRUCTIVE ANTHROPOLOGY

One of my earliest memories is of a totem pole. Living just around the corner from the Museum of the American Indian—then located on the Upper West Side of Manhattan—the massive totem pole that sat in the museum's courtyard cast a shadow over my early childhood. The museum was an enchanted place, with its colorful artifacts, and its carefully constructed dioramas of Native American life. It was there that my fascination with anthropology was born.

In my early teens I decided I wanted to be an ethno-musicologist, in order to pursue my interest in folk music.

But as I became more involved in the anti-war movement and radical politics in my later teen years, I dismissed anthropology as an indulgence, and focused instead on political science and history, believing that the revolution required more practical knowledge than could be gleaned from the study of such exotic and frivolous subject matter as that approached by anthropology.

When I was in my early twenties, as I pursued my interest in anarchism and social ecology, I was confronted, as I have been at many points in my life, by my own ignorance. My understanding was limited by my background, which was that of a recent college graduate who had led a largely middle class existence. As a child of the '60s, I had been caught up in the excitement of the anti-war movement and the counterculture, but my experience during those heady times had been primarily visceral, not informed by intensive study or research. Though more motivated by the desire to solidify a theoretical basis for effective action than by a love of scholarship for the sake of scholarship, I felt the need to deepen my understanding of the dynamics of cultural change, and the human prospect. So I returned to anthropology: it was the only academic discipline I was aware of that allowed its practitioners to consider the whole range of the human experience throughout the whole of human history and pre-history. It was both pan-human, and transhistorical in its outlook; it was not limited to the study of the here and now, and, while still a discipline born of the Western experience, theoretically, at least, it drew on all of the world's cultures to provide insight into their commonalities as well as their differences.

As such, anthropology can offer a vital perspective into how other cultures have organized themselves without the market or the state, it calls into question the inevitability of capitalism, and it helps to illuminate human potential. Anthropological understanding certainly helps us to remove the blinders of the western cannon: I believe it can help to combat racism, give insight into the process of cultural change, and serve as an invaluable knowledge base for a revolutionary project.

The Crisis in Anthropology

However, when I began my graduate studies in the late 1960s, I quickly discovered that anthropology was in crisis. Anthropologists were engaged in a serious critique of their discipline: the post-colonial era was raising questions regarding anthropology's origins and purpose, and the theoretical firmament provided by Franz Boas and Claude Levi-Strauss was being shaken by challenges from new theories, like cultural materialism and the emerging ideas of post-structuralism. By the 1970s, when I was writing my dissertation, the upheavals that shook the discipline in the '60s had receded, but the questions remained pertinent, as they still remain today. What relevance does anthropology have in the increasingly specialized world of "social science"? Where does a discipline born from the study of "primitive" cultures turn when those cultures disappear? How can anthropology resist its use as an instrument of domination and become, instead, a force for liberation and reconstruction? As a newly minted anthropologist I was deeply troubled by these questions, and I have continued to struggle with them for the past thirty years. Even though I have earned my living as an anthropologist, I have always maintained an ambivalent and marginal relationship to professional anthropology, which led me to try to formulate some ideas that might help me to address these questions. These ideas, I hope, will provide food for thought and stimulate further development—they are meant to be more suggestive than prescriptive—in order to counter the crisis in anthropology.

The crisis in anthropology unfolded on three distinct but related levels—professional, theoretical, and ethical. Professionally, anthropologists found that their traditional objects of study were no longer readily available to them: The so-called "primitive societies," "tribal society," "kin-based society," "pre-literate society," or "traditional societies," as I prefer, by which I mean societies, groups, and cultures that exist outside of the reach of, or at the margins of, the rapidly expanding realm of global capitalism, and retain much of their historic tradition and cosmology. The decimation of these traditional societies has been proceeding at an exponential rate, and as the natural environments that provide the material base for those societies—such as the rain forests, the arctic regions, and vast tracts of undeveloped land needed to support hunting and gathering and traditional nomadic pastoralism—are increasingly being destroyed and eroded, so are traditional societies themselves. We can only expect an acceleration of these trends.

Just as scientists recognize the threats to survival represented by the destruction of natural environments and the extinction of species, anthropologists have warned of the dangers posed by the destruction of cultures and their knowledge. The frightening loss of biodiversity that we are facing is paralleled by an equally frightening destruction of cultural diversity, as the homogenizing effects of global capitalism accelerate throughout the world.

Furthermore, traditional societies that have gained their liberation from colonial relationships have become increasingly suspicious of, and in some cases hostile to, the anthropological enterprise. They often associate anthropology with colonialism and paternalism. Justified as this attitude is, given the historical record, anthropology is nothing if not adaptable: its terrain is the study of people and their cultures in all of their broad dimensions throughout the whole of history.

Recognizing the practical and political problems facing conventional types of study, many anthropologists, myself among them, shifted their focus to the anthropology of "modern" societies. We engaged in urban studies, migration studies, family studies, community studies, and in applied anthropology. But here too, we are faced with a crisis in traditional ethnographic methods that have largely proved inadequate for the task of analyzing groups in the context of the larger culture of capitalism in which they must be placed. In these fields, anthropology has often lost its unique, holistic approach to become instead a reductive, instrumental field, really just a qualitative adjunct to sociology, narrow in scope, specialized to the point of a focus on social minutiae and divorced from the culture concept itself. Historically, however, anthropology has always concerned itself with questions that are of great import to understanding our human past, the dynamics of social change, and human prospects and possibilities for the future. Anthropology has addressed big questions like, what is culture? How does cultural change occur? What constitutes human "nature"? In an era of increasing academic specialization, these larger concerns seem to have fallen by the wayside.

In some cases, research in professional anthropology is being constricted and contorted by more general trends in the academy that limit funding to research projects that meet the needs of an increasingly reactionary status quo. Many anthropology departments in the United States have disappeared altogether or been collapsed into departments of sociology. Add to this the fact that the majority of anthropology PhDs will never work in the academy and face highly limited job possibilities in nonacademic fields relating to anthropology. Recently *The Chronicle of Higher Education* surveyed the job market in anthropology and determined that 50% of the almost 500 PhDs graduated in the US each year—that includes anthropologists working in all four fields of anthropology: biological anthropology, anthropological linguistics, archeology, and ethnography— will end up employed in the government or private sector, working in consulting, public relations, opinion poling, banking and finance, or federal and state law enforcement. Only a few of those who do work in the academy will end up with tenure-track positions, and the rest will be consigned to the growing pool of visiting professors, lecturers, and adjuncts who constitute the new, flexible labor force required by the education business. The situation for ethnographers in particular is even worse than these statistics suggest. When these facts are added together, one has the profile of a profession in deep trouble.

On a theoretical level the crisis is more subtle, but no less profound. The basic theoretical divide in anthropology has always been between those who approach it as a science and those who view it as a branch of the humanities. This dispute has never been resolved. Despite a multitude of competing theoretical frameworks, very little coherence has emerged beyond theories propounded over specific problems. Indeed, the theoretical debate within anthropology has been stifled by the ascendency of several major positions, which are seemingly irreconcilable. Each has developed a cadre of proponents who exercise a stranglehold on particular fields of anthropology and who seem determined to perpetuate their own outlook. A theoretical base, broad enough to explain cultural change, traditional ethnographic data, and contemporary social problems, is not likely to achieve consensus in the current climate of ideologically loaded discourse. Furthermore, many anthropologists operate without an explicit theoretical framework, and this tendency has been strengthened alongside an increased focus on social minutiae rather than more comprehensive cultural analysis.. These anthropologists may argue for "scientific objectivity," or, in the case of postmodernists and post-structuralists, attempt to operate from a completely relativistic mindset. But, by refusing to define a theoretical position, they are in fact accepting the underlying premises of the dominant ideology: it is impossible to escape entirely one's background and cultural conditioning.

Dominant Trends in Academic Anthropology

Before we turn to the ethical crisis in anthropology, let us briefly review some of the dominant theories in academic anthropology then and now, and quickly summarize the salient critiques that have been offered of them.

At the turn of the last century, Franz Boas developed his historical particularism—also known as Boasian relativism—which became an important theoretical development in anthropology, with its recognition of the intrinsic integrity of every culture and its self-conscious stance in combating racism. However, in its reaction to nineteenth-century evolutionary models, Boasian relativism presented a static view of culture and lacked an explicit perspective for explaining cultural change. Much of the focus of Boas and his students, whose influence on modern American anthropology is still felt today, was the undertaking of "salvage ethnography," an attempt to observe and describe threatened traditional cultures, like those of Native American peoples, before they vanished altogether.

Then, in the 1950s, Claude Levi-Strauss established structuralism, which emerged as an influential perspective in anthropology that attempted to discover universal principles of the human mind that underlay cultural traits, customs, and myths. The theory drew on concepts developed in linguistics, and it likened the structures of cultures to the structures of language. Levi-Strauss's theory was influential, and useful in helping to identify the underlying unity of all cultures, but it was utterly unable to explain cultures as distinct and particular entities with highly diverse content and unique differences. Structuralists claim a pan-human application for their theory, but what is ultimately revealed is structure without content—it is a lowest-common-denominator approach to cultural analysis which conceals more than it explicates. The structuralists, it seems, simply ignore society to focus on its "structures." Specific manifestations of a culture are seen as less important than the broad categories that all cultures share. Structuralism, in turn, lay the groundwork for other theoretical schools, such as symbolic anthropology, cognitive anthropology, and, importantly, postmodernism.

In the 1960s and 1970s, Marxism had a tremendous influence in anthropology. But, unfortunately, it was often introduced as a rigid framework for analysis that contorted on-the-ground experience to fit into predetermined categories of little relevance to the reality of traditional people. Marx and Engels themselves drew heavily on the work of early anthropologists like Lewis Henry Morgan to develop their understanding of cultural evolution. Morgan's schema was deeply flawed in its emphasis on cultural evolution as social Darwinism, but Marxism itself is, in fact, an extremely deterministic ideology that places an inordinate—and historically unjustifiable—faith in inexorable historical processes and "progress."

Cultural ecology was the phrase used by Julian Steward to describe his theory of cultural evolution, a much more nuanced approach than the crude theories of the nineteenth century evolutionists and Social Darwinists. Steward used what was essentially a Marxist framework, but he emphasized environmental causality as the underlying factor creating cultural adaptation and change, rather than economic factors.

On the other hand, cultural materialism, as practiced by anthropologists like Marvin Harris, constituted a reduction and further vulgarization of the Marxist view. While it was suggestive and sometimes productive for analyzing cultural change, this scientistic perspective fails to incorporate symbolic, cosmological, or psychological causality into these schemas. Rather, it reduces all cultural phenomena to an interaction between land, labor, and capital; specific cultural traits are seen as an obfuscation of the underlying reasons for change, which are presented as mere responses to environmental factors.

From the 1980s on, two major theoretical schools emerged, which highlight the long-standing divide between anthropology as a science, and anthropology as a branch of the humanities.

One the one hand, we saw how the tendency toward anthropological scientism found new proponents with the emergence of sociobiological anthropology, a theoretical approach which attempts to explain human behavior from a biological perspective, with a major emphasis on the role of genes in creating universal forms of human behavior. Sociobiological anthropologists focus on three main categories of study: evolutionary biology, human behavioral ecology, and the study of human universals. For sociobiological anthropologists, human behavior and culture are essentially genetic functions that, in a Darwinian sense, either aid or hinder reproductive success. This extremely reductive view fails to consider the crucial role of culture, and often draws on research with non-human populations, like insects, and projects these results onto human populations.

By biologizing every aspect of human behavior, this approach denies any role for ethics, education, and a myriad of other cultural phenomena that influence the direction in which communities evolve.

On the other hand, we saw how the postmodern, post-structuralist turn in anthropology called science into question altogether, maintaining, at its most extreme, that there is no such thing as a scientific fact or even objective reality. It proposes, rather, that facts are cultural constructs, and that reality is a relative concept. Postmodernism presents a useful perspective for an ethnographer, demanding that, to the extent possible, the anthropologist approach a culture on its own terms. It also presents powerful insights in deconstructing power relationships, noting how a position of cultural hegemony allows one group to dictate reality for others.

However, postmodernism also represents a real danger: the assumption of such an extreme relativism makes it impossible to make ethical judgments, and it easily leads to quietism in the face of oppression and domination.

These theoretical perspectives are seemingly irreconcilable. Where, then, can anthropology turn for a theoretical framework that integrates processual understanding and structural commonalities, and yet still recognizes the unique, particularistic aspects of specific cultures? Is there a theory that allows us to understand the process of cultural change without hierarchical schema for valuing different cultures? Is there a way to draw on scientific understanding without being reductive? In order to fully address and hopefully resolve the current crisis in anthropology, we must first outline the ethical dimension of this crisis.

As an academic discipline anthropology positions itself as a "value-free" approach to the study of culture. This was true of Boasian historical particularism, and it is even more true in the era of post-structuralism. Important as this was in response to nineteenth century evolutionism and Social Darwinism, I would nonetheless argue that a "value-free" approach to the study of culture and society is simply not possible. What then are the values that anthropology reflects? Unfortunately—and inevitably, I would add, given the lack of a clear theoretical orientation—for the most part they have been the values of the dominant culture, our own.

Both consciously and unconsciously anthropology has served as a handmaiden of domination and exploitation. Historically, anthropologists have provided strategic information for those who have exploited and colonized the people whom anthropologists have studied. In a very real sense, the earliest ethnographers were not academic anthropologists, but rather conquistadores, colonial administrators and the clergy who accompanied them. The information that they provided was used to expand and maintain control over subjugated people. In USA, there is also a long history of anthropologists collaborating with the military and the CIA, from World War II, with the creation of departments of area studies to aid the war effort, through Vietnam, and into our own time. To be sure, professional anthropology has a code of ethics stating that "prior to making any professional commitments, they must review the purposes of employers, taking into consideration the employers past activities and future goals. In working for government agencies or private business they should be especially careful not to promise or imply conditions contrary to professional ethics or competing commitments." Further, anthropologists "must consider carefully the social and political implications of information they disseminate." and they "must be alert to possible harm their information may cause people with whom they work or their colleagues." This ethical code was toughened in 2009 in reaction to the news that anthropologists had been working with the US military in Iraq and Afghanistan, though it still does not explicitly forbid secret research for the military or the more widespread—and growing—practice of undertaking proprietary research for corporations. Despite a growing awareness of this dimension of anthropology, these relationships still persist. As noted earlier, this is clearly one of the symptoms of the professional crisis facing anthropology as a discipline.

Aside from those who knowingly collaborate, anthropologists of all types—traditional ethnographers, those engaged in urban studies, and particularly applied anthropologists—find themselves serving, willingly or unwillingly, as "fact finders" for those who would homogenize the world's cultures, providing insight into belief systems and social organization that can be, and are, easily used by states and corporate actors to develop strategies for controlling and dominating the people being studied. Once their research is made public, anthropologists have no control over how it is used. This ethical dilemma is unavoidable in current anthropological practice unless one consciously defines oneself in opposition to the culture of domination and exploitation.

Given the pervasive nature of these interrelated crises what is the way out? Is there a perspective that can help anthropology reshape itself as a coherent, ethical discipline that has relevance to the critical problems faced by our civilization and our planet? I believe that the answer is an unequivocal yes; further, I would suggest that the elements needed for such a reshaping are largely present in the anthropological tradition itself. We need to develop an anthropology that is self-conscious about its role in both observing and shaping culture, an anthropology that is both critical and utopian—in short, a reconstructive anthropology.

Where in the anthropological corpus do we find the elements we need to draw together toward this end? What are the preconditions for a synthesis? I wish to suggest that the elements we need can be drawn selectively from three distinct approaches to anthropology: critical anthropology, social ecology, and participatory action research. But before we turn to a more detailed examination of how we might constitute a reconstructive anthropology, we must explore its preconditions.

The Critical Dimension

Regarding philosophy, Hegel declared that "The owl of Minerva always flies at dusk." We might say as much of anthropology. Why do our insights into cultures, their values, their organizational forms and, particularly, their process of change usually come only after destructive change has already occurred? Are we incapable of predicting changes? Do we favor them? Or is it that we do not care? I would answer no to all of these questions: The owl of Minerva flies at dusk because of our conceptualization of anthropology as a descriptive, analytical, and reflective discipline.

This is of course not meant to suggest that description, analysis and reflection are bad. On the contrary, they remain *necessary* aspects of the anthropological enterprise, but, from the perspective of reconstructive anthropology, they are *not sufficient*. In order to address the ethical dilemma of anthropology, as indicated earlier, we must start by consciously identifying ourselves with the objects of our study. In so doing we transcend the dichotomy between subject and object to establish a relationship of intersubjectivity, and anthropology becomes not only a reflective discipline but also an *interactive* one. The crucial identification with the "objects" of study and the establishment of truly intersubjective relationships are necessary components to insure that the anthropology we practice is reconstructive in nature and not simply an instrumental application of anthropological perspectives.

It is interesting to note here that anthropology has always concerned itself with humanely scaled communities that function in a relatively unmediated fashion: Typical examples are the hunting and gathering band; pastoral peoples, both nomadic and sedentary; peasant farming communities; and, more recently, ethnic neighborhoods and sub-cultural enclaves. Anthropologists have focused on societies and cultures where face-to-face interactions are the dominant mode of relationship. The very intimacy of these groups makes them more approachable, and more conducive to the primary mode of research utilized by cultural anthropologists, that of participation and observation. As such, they also present situations in which it is possible to create truly intersubjective relationships.

There exists within anthropology a tradition that had always been based on the principle of intersubjectivity. Stanley Diamond identifies this tradition as "critical anthropology" and counterposes this outlook to the increasing scientism of academic anthropology. For Diamond, critical anthropology is concerned with the study of the "primitive," in order to illuminate our understanding of ourselves, and to expand our understanding of what constitutes the human potential.

The modern anthropological project, Diamond argues, saw an early manifestation of this tradition in Jean-Jacques Rousseau's concern with "primitive society" and "man in nature," and in his use of the comparative model, notably, of the state versus civil society. For Diamond, this comparative perspective is the essence of critical anthropology. What can traditional cultures tell us about our own society—its origins and its prospects? Diamond creates a paradigm he called "the primitive/civilized dichotomy," that brings into bold relief the qualitative differences between cultures organized around the principles of reciprocity, mutualism and participation, and those organized around the market, the state, and the compartmentalization of its members. Diamond's dichotomy— which I suggest is best understood as a continuum—helps us to broaden our understanding of "human nature," or, more properly, human potential, by contrasting the forms of social organization, ranging from egalitarian to authoritarian, utilized by different cultures. Diamond shows how various social formations reinforce and reward particular aspects of "human nature" and de-value others.

With the establishment of academic anthropology these crucial issues were frequently subsumed under the rubric of cultural relativism. This tendency eschews comparison for a cultural leveling which, while it combats racism and help us to value all cultures, serves at the same time to blind us to the qualitative differences that do exist between cultures—I do not mean to suggest a qualitative *ranking* of cultures here, but a recognition of their qualitatively different existential experiences. Diamond, however, insists that a critical tradition in anthropology has always been present within the discipline. He identifies this tradition with the work of people like Paul Radin, Marshal Sahlins, Eric Wolfe, Dell Hymes, Pierre Clastres, and others. By extension one could argue that the emergence of feminist anthropology is part of this tradition.

Critical anthropology calls for the self-examination of the fieldwork as an integral part of the anthropological project. Diamond also calls for the conscious identification of the field worker with his or her object of study—a radical position indeed. Still, even with its emphasis on this identification, the praxis of critical anthropology remained primarily an intellectual enterprise: it was scholarship oriented toward an important end—self-understanding—but still merely scholarship and abstractly conceptual.

Diamond's goals were explicit; he saw the need for "a cultural transformation as profound as the shift from the Neolithic to civilization" and suggested that critical anthropologists must become partisans in struggles for liberation and for social reconstruction. What forms can this partnership take? What, beyond scholarship, is the *practice* of critical anthropology? How does critical anthropology become interactive beyond the level of theory?

Surely, anthropology has always had an interactive dimension, although it has not always been conscious, and only in rare cases has it been critical. In many cases, this interaction has offered the use of anthropological studies and data in the process of subjugating and assimilating cultures and communities by the dominant culture. Often, anthropologists are unconscious of the uses to which their research is applied, but in some cases there has been conscious collaboration.

Most work done under the rubric of "applied anthropology" provides negative examples of anthropological interaction. Most applied work occurs in concert with the forces of domination, be they capitalist or "socialist." Applied anthropology has mitigated some of the overt brutality of this cultural imperialism but it has nonetheless played an important role in assimilating unique communities into the larger political and economic structures of the dominant culture.

Anthropology that interacts on the level of policy design which is intended to assimilate traditional people into modern nation-states—or plans the pacification of dissident communities—crosses the line from the unconsciously to the consciously evil. At this level anthropology loses its humanistic content, as well as any pretense of "scientific objectivity." In these cases anthropology has become an instrument for the destruction of the very thing that had sustained it, the ultimate parasite.

As currently constituted, much of applied anthropology falls into this category. It has lacked both critical content and self-consciousness. The work of applied anthropology has to be reoriented toward the support of traditional, alternative, and oppositional cultural movements—all of which are under assault by the forces of domination and homogeneity. If applied anthropology is to provide elements for a reconstructive synthesis its intentionality must be inverted. We must create a critical applied anthropology that identifies with the culture under assault, helps to develop strategies for cultural survival, and expands resistance rather than adaptation and assimilation.

Participatory Action and Community

There is a methodology that explicitly requires such a level of engagement: participatory action research. This is a collaborative process in which the researcher works actively with community members to examine problems in their community that they wish to address, and develop action in order to change or improve them. It requires critical analysis of all relevant political, cultural, historical, economic, and environmental factors that contributed to creating the problem. As the name indicates, participatory action research is a process of action as much as it is a process of description, analysis, and reflection: it constitutes an ongoing praxis, an action that is analyzed, modified, and then redeployed.

In other words, anthropologists should ally themselves with a particular community as a *resource* for that community. They must share their insight with the community, helping people to analyze and interpret their own situation with the explicit goal of maintaining or perhaps reconstructing cultural traditions that support the cultural integrity of that community. As I see it, reconstructive anthropology must engage in the planning process as well: not by implementing the top-down planning mechanisms of the dominant culture, but rather by encouraging and taking part in a participatory planning process in which the community itself determines its future direction. This process must therefore, in part, be an educational endeavor that helps to ensure that a community takes conscious, critical choices about its future. Paolo Freire, who has done much to inspire this participatory approach, describes in his *Pedagogy of the Oppressed* how a community can learn its way together to deal with problems. Such a process inverts the usual planning mechanisms in which applied anthropology plays a role.

In light of this, the involvement of anthropologists in these communities and their struggles has another important dimension as well: to fully eclipse the subject/object dichotomy it is necessary to establish active solidarity. Reconstructive anthropology must be rooted in *engagement* and—if intersubjectivity is to be created—*reciprocity*. Here I do not mean the payment of "informants" for their time and information, nor a reductive quid pro quo, but rather the deeper sense of reciprocity, as expressed by traditional people: active involvement in the lives and struggles of those with whom we work. Indeed, reciprocity in the deepest sense is not an economic form: it is not a relationship of exchange, based on the calculation of return-in-kind. It is *mutualistic*, growing out of a sensibility of solidarity—an organic interrelationship in which the action of each supports the other—and a recognition that the whole is greater than the sum of its parts. Such mutualism, I would argue, is a vital principle: anything less is parasitic and paternalistic, as the trajectory of anthropology has shown. Academic anthropologists have traditionally built their careers from work with "their people" and returned little or nothing. The interaction of anthropology and the process of cultural and community reconstruction also has implications for the professional crisis in anthropology. Anthropological training should not be limited to use in the classroom or placed in the service of state and corporate entities. The work of the reconstructive anthropologist lies in the world—in communities and neighborhoods where people are struggling to control their lives. The reconstructive anthropologist may have to look beyond the traditional avenues of employment, but the opportunities to actively practice reconstructive anthropology are numerous. Anthropology must be understood as a calling, not a narrow vocation. The sensibility of reconstructive anthropology demands praxis.

Praxis, to be complete, is not confined to action, however, or even action informed by an anthropological perspective. It requires action in a dialectical relationship with a theoretical perspective: a fluid coupling in which each component consistently interacts with and reshapes the other. For the reconstructive approach to become a potent force in the world we need to overcome not only the ethical and professional crisis in anthropology, but the theoretical crisis as well. If we believe that a critical approach is needed to address the basic orientation of anthropology and that a critical applied anthropology can open creative paths for dealing with professional limitations, where can we turn for an adequate grounding in theory?

The Promise of Social Ecology

While there are a myriad of theories that have utility for specific questions raised in anthropology, one outlook provides a framework that addresses the major issues with real coherence and consistency: social ecology. The theoretical insights of social ecology are uniquely suited to the new synthesis required if a reconstructive anthropology is to emerge.

Social ecology must be distinguished from the reductive cultural materialism, cultural ecology and other such forms of "ecological" theory currently in vogue in the academy. Social ecology focuses on the relationship between society and nature; indeed it posits this relationship as central for cultural change, but in a multilineal fashion that integrates nonmaterial elements into the causal mix. Anthropology, as we have seen, is tormented by its conflicts between science and the humanities. Social ecology, in its nuanced concepts of "first" and "second" nature, strikes a balance between the two domains, by emphasizing the role of natural evolution— what it calls "first nature"—in creating the biological basis for human life and community, and the gradual emergence out of first nature of a range of cultural factors that, while still a product of first nature, represent a qualitative change—a "second nature"—that allows a culture to alter direction dramatically in less than a generation. Social ecology, at its most profound level, offers these insights not as a rigid ideology or dogma, but rather as a framework for inquiry that is explicitly oriented toward reharmonizing people's relationship with the natural world. Further, social ecology suggests an ethics that can inform decisions about the kind of commitments that reconstructive anthropologists make.

A recurring theme in social ecology is the relationship between the domination of nature and the domination of people. Murray Bookchin, the foremost theorist of social ecology, sees the elimination of the domination of people by other people as a precondition for the reharmonization of people and the natural world. The theory examines theas well aspossible , and evaluates cosmology, technics, environmental factors, and social organization as causal factors in the dialectics of culture and nature.

Social Ecology is concerned with the evolutionary process that explicates our contemporary civilization's destructive relationships to both the natural world and the social world in order to suggest reconstructive approaches. This theory attempts to present a critical and utopian view that can help us make sense of the world, and suggests the transcendental dimension inherent in a reconstructive anthropology. Unlike vulgar variants of ecological theory, such as cultural materialism, social ecology is coherent without being schematic or dogmatic. On the contrary, it emphasizes the uniqueness of each culture it examines and has an explicitly libratory intent. Understood as an open system of inquiry, social ecology's framework has proven invaluable for me, and many others. However, it is also an evolving theory and has many gaps which anthropology can help to address.

By focusing on ecological relationships in both the realm of nature and culture, social ecology presents a paradigm that illuminates prehistory and contemporary society. It demonstrates the development of the latter out of the former, but it does so in a critical manner that calls into question the presuppositions of progress and linearity that underlie civilization's sense of its own development. Social Ecology consciously addresses the most pressing problems facing the planet—the domination and exploitation of people and cultures, pollution, resource depletion, agricultural collapse, destructive patterns of development, technological determinism, climate change, and the threat of nuclear war— all from an anthropological perspective. Indeed, as I see it, it constitutes the theoretical perspective needed to formalize a reconstructive anthropology. To be more specific, social ecology suggests that the creative human enterprise, when informed by a conscious understanding of the relationship between culture and nature, can create a new level of culture, profoundly different from our current civilization, free from hierarchy and domination, and in harmony with the other species on this planet.

The ethics of social ecology are derived from an interpretation of natural evolution that emphasizes the role of non-hierarchical relationships, mutualism, unity in diversity, homeostasis, spontaneity, and ever greater degrees of consciousness and freedom in the evolutionary process: it suggests that these same principles must be developed as an ethical basis for action in the social realm if we are to ever achieve a healthy, ecological society. The ethics of social ecology thus provide a powerful set of ethical guidelines for the work of reconstructive anthropology.

Toward a Reconstructive Anthropology

What, then, are the implications of a reconstructive anthropology? What are the concrete tasks that practitioners of such an approach might undertake? Not unlike academic anthropology, a primary task of the reconstructive approach is the delineation of the process of cultural evolution with particular emphasis on the emergence of hierarchy, domination and the state. Reconstructive anthropology must examine this development in relation to particular cultures and, departing significantly from academic anthropology, must do so with the explicit goal not only of explication but also of *transformation*. Beyond offering insight into the roots of class stratification and state formation, it must consciously link the anthropologist with the project of human liberation and ecological restoration by suggesting concrete alternatives to contemporary hierarchical social relations and ecologically destructive social practices. As such, reconstructive anthropology must be understood as a perspective and a project that transcends the given of a narrowly defined human nature in order to, in the words of anthropologist David Graeber, "understand the human condition and move it in the direction of greater freedom."

This concern must be fully integrated into the forms that the practice of reconstructive anthropology takes: First of all in the *content* of our studies, which focus on questions of significance to a ecological and emancipatory perspective, as well as in the *intentionality* of our work, which implies active collaboration with communities and movements working for ecologically oriented human liberation. It must also be manifest in our focus on *intersubjective relationships* rather than the classical dichotomy between subject and object. As I see it, a concern with hierarchy and domination is by no means the only appropriate topic for investigation, but it must be integrated fully into a perspective that informs our work as a whole.

In a world of increasingly fragmented bits of knowledge, reconstructive anthropology offers a holistic framework for analysis, critique and praxis. That framework can be used to explore particular problems of concern to a given community: economic development, environmental degradation, land reform, family relations, health care, technology diffusion, agricultural development; indeed, the list can encompass every aspect of a culture. But the method of reconstructive anthropology requires an integrative approach that places the particular problem examined within a multi-causal matrix in dialectical tension with the whole of the culture.

The method proceeds through distinct stages of analysis and action: there are cultural and historical research and reflection, analysis of the contemporary situation, critique, planning and development of alternative models, action and implementation, evolution, incorporation of experience into new theoretical models, and further action—all prompted by participation as well as observation. The method must be participatory and inclusive, where the anthropologist serves as a resource and, to the extent possible, as a catalyst throughout the process. This intersubjective relationship provides a basis of love, trust, and mutual respect necessary for an effective reconstructive praxis.

It is surely a departure from "objective" scientific approaches of anthropology to ask for love, trust and mutual respect as inherent methodological components for praxis. However, I maintain that these qualities are necessary parts of any process that hopes to change the basic nature of the dominant culture. Without these underlying ethical relationships, no authentic cultural reconstruction can occur. I call for their development and implementation not as abstract concepts but as crucial existential reality, as an ethical sensibility that can provide grounding for the work of reconstruction.

The methodology of reconstructive anthropology suggests that the most appropriate place for the reconstructive anthropologist to work is in his or her own culture—perhaps even his or her own community. In this regard, the theory of the "marginal man" as agent of cultural change, proposed by Louis Wirth of the Chicago School, bears examination.

Wirth suggested that the individual with a foot in two cultures, the person who is at the margins of his or her own society and has experienced a culture foreign to him or her, is the one who is most effective at introducing new concepts and cultural innovations. Growing out of cultural cross-fertilization, such marginal individuals exhibit a genius for cultural experimentation, and yet they are familiar enough with the existent conditions to be socially creative.

Ultimately, who is more marginal than the anthropologist? Anthropology is itself a marginal discipline within the academy. Individuals who choose to study anthropology are notorious for their idiosyncratic behavior and their social marginality, and they often come from multicultural backgrounds or have had multicultural experiences. And this personal marginality is reinforced further by the study of anthropology: indeed solidified by the field experience— unique to anthropology—of being a participant/observer. Those drawn to reconstructive anthropology further confirm their marginal status by choosing a marginal—practically non-existent—trajectory within a marginal discipline. The reconstructive anthropologist seems to be the marginal person par excellence and, if Wirth is correct, potentially an effective agent for cultural change.

There are an increasing number of people studying anthropology who come from communities that have traditionally been the subjects of anthropological research. Some, like my late friend John Mohawk in the Akwasasenee Mohawk community, or Gustavo Esteve working in Oaxaca, have been able to apply their anthropological understanding in reconstructive projects in their own communities. This encouraging development suggests to me that one goal of reconstructive anthropology should be educating more people from diverse backgrounds in the theories and techniques of the reconstructive approach. I believe that the most effective practitioners will be those who work in their own communities.

The marginal stance of reconstructive anthropology is further enhanced by the need for its practitioners to develop a propensity for what Paul Goodman called "utopian thinking"—the ability to project beyond the given to what could be. This conceptualization of *what could be* cannot remain an individual vision. It needs to be teased out by means of a participatory communal process that evokes the aspirations of the communities we work with. It cannot be a "blueprint"—it must grow out of a utopian process, indeed out of the praxis of reconstructive anthropology as such, in all of its existential and ethical wealth of experience.

In some cases anthropologists may play a therapeutic social role, aiding a given community or culture to transcend the forces of fragmentation that contribute to cultural neurosis and psychosis. This is almost analogous to the role that the psychotherapist plays in relation to the individual, but reconstructive anthropology must be informed by a radical ethical intentionality—not an adaptive one—in order to create wholeness and integrity: the very integration that is the hallmark of traditional cultures.

In this way anthropologists draws on cross-cultural, transhistorical insights to extract principles necessary for the creation of healthy communities and finally, through a process of dialectical transformation, reintegrates those principles into the institutions and relationships of his or her own community. This process can occur through the reinforcement of still-existing traditions, through the revitalization of vestigial forms, or even through the creation of new institutional, organizational, and relational forms.

Decentralization and Human Scale

Reconstructive anthropology is by necessity rooted in decentralization and an appreciation of human scale. A global perspective must inform the concerns of reconstructive anthropology, but its practical approach must proceed locally—at the grassroots level—if the transformative development is to be authentic. Community can only be built and sustained through participation; it rests on primary relationships, and on face to face ties, which require a human scale. To be sure, humanly scaled communities have always been the subject of anthropological reflection: Anthropology—even academic anthropology—has always claimed this terrain as its own, and it represents a vital part of the anthropological tradition which must be retained by the reconstructive approach. The "little community," the village, the neighborhood, and the intentional community: these are the realms of action for reconstructive anthropology. Community provides the basis for cultural and ecological revitalization and change.

These are at least three broad areas in which reconstructive anthropology must be practiced. First, I would argue, we must work with tribal and traditional cultures confronted by the homogenizing effects of modernity. Second, we must vitalize community development efforts in existing communities. Finally, we must stimulate the creation of new intentional communities and alternative ways of living. While the examples are few and far between, exciting work is currently done in all of these areas that relates to the ethical framework suggested for a reconstructive anthropology.

Reconstructive anthropology holds great promise. While anthropology as a discipline seems to have schemes of "value-free," the goal of a reconstructive anthropology is to engage the human spirit, to stimulate the human imagination in order to help in the unfolding of the human potential, and to provide a reconstructive, ethical basis for human community.

ALTERNATIVE TECHNOLOGY AND URBAN RECONSTRUCTION

We are living in the new era of "green." Green technologies like solar, wind, biomass, and co-generation are being presented as the solution to climate change, our dependence on foreign oil, and the economic crisis. We are told that green jobs are the jobs of the future. Ideas and technologies that were once the province of radical ecologists and the counterculture have entered the mainstream, and large transnational corporations are scrambling to jump aboard the bandwagon. BP, formely British Petroleum, recently marketed itself as "Beyond Petroleum." Greenwashing is the order of the day.

"Green Cities" are all the rage. The new interest in, and policy shift toward encouraging the use of alternative technologies, like solar energy and wind power, in urban environments—along with a growing emphasis on urban farming, energy efficiency, green architecture, green planning, and all things local—is unprecedented. Or is it?

In the late 1970s the Hispanic section of New York City's Lower East Side, known to its Puerto Rican Residents as Loisaida, grassroots efforts at community development utilized all of these approaches and more. In light of the newfound emphasis on green technology as the force that will move us into the future, these remarkable efforts seem prescient, and further examination might prove instructive.

I was privileged to be a part of these experiments, through my work with the Institute for Social Ecology (ISE), and my involvement with CHARAS, a group of young activists and community organizers who played a critical role in the developments in Loisaida. I first became aware of this work in 1974 when I organized a conference on urban alternatives in New York City. We brought together urban activists and green technology innovators like John Todd of the New Alchemy Institute, Karl Hess from the Adams-Morgan neighborhood in Washington, Milton Kotler, author of *Neighborhood Government,* wind energy developer Ted Finch, and urban gardener Tessa Huxley. Following the conference I was approached by grassroots activists from Loisaida and asked if the Institute for Social Ecology could provide technical and program planning assistance.

The ISE worked on a variety of projects with the 11th Street Movement, the Cultural Understanding and

Neighborhood Development Organization (CUANDO), and CHARAS, helping in planning of programs and the design of specific projects related to solar energy, wind power, aquaculture, and urban gardening. I was living in New York at the time, and began to work intensely with the Lower East Side groups as a volunteer consultant. We developed a relationship of reciprocity, where groups of ISE students came to New York to help with projects in Loisaida, and members of the Loisaida groups came to Vermont to help us with our projects. An intersubjective relationship based in solidarity, mutual respect, and affection developed which forged strong relationships that persist to this day.

As my involvement deepened I became fascinated with the projects and convinced of their importance as an application of many of the ideas and technologies that we worked with at the ISE. I was studying Cultural Anthropology at the New School for Social Research and I decided to write my doctoral dissertation about Loisaida. My thesis focused on the role of alternative or green technology in grassroots efforts at Loisaida's neighborhood reconstruction. The reconstruction undertaken was both cultural and physical. The people of Loisaida were people in transition, seeking a new, ecological lifestyle. It was a cultural expression with many sources: rooted in a strong traditional Puerto Rican culture, it was an adaptation to the conditions of life in the ghetto, and also a response to the mass culture of global capitalism. Above all, it was an experiment in urban survival. The experience of Loisaida has much to teach us all. While I was able to offer insights and bring skills to the process, I readily admit that I learned much more than I taught.

Alternative Technology

A group of Loisaida residents was the first low-income group of urban dwellers in the United States to attempt utilizing alternative technology in the reconstruction of their community. They used ecologically sound organic gardening and aquaculture techniques to reintroduce food production to New York City. They developed low-cost ways to use solar energy to meet their energy needs, and they began to recycle the wastes that littered their neighborhood into resources for development. They pioneered the transformation of abandoned buildings into affordable tenant-owned cooperative housing through the process of urban homesteading. Ultimately, they began to create forms of social and political organization through which they tried to regain control of their lives and neighborhood.

The alternative technology movement in the 1970s and '80s was largely the province of middle-class people of a counter-cultural persuasion. The involvement of this low-income, mostly Puerto Rican community was indeed a significant development.

During that period technologies based on utilizing renewable energy sources were known by a variety of names: radical, soft, alternative, or appropriate technology. In general, they were understood as those technologies which are small scale and relatively simple, and therefore useful for decentralized application, based on the use of non-polluting, renewable energy sources; they were tailored to utilize locally available resources, both for construction materials and labor in a manner which supports, or at least does not disrupt, local cultural patterns and enhances local self-reliance.

Alternative technology was first applied in relation to developing nations as an alternative to capital-intensive models of Western development. By the mid 1970s, there was a growing interest in the application of these technologies to the developed world, as a means of alleviating our dependence on fossil fuels and the concurrent ecological costs of that dependence.

The advocates of this technological approach were arrayed on a continuum ranging from those who advocated the incorporation of alternative technology into existing capitalist modes of production, such as E.F. Schumacher, to those who saw these technologies as part of a more fundamental transformation of our society into a decentralized, non-hierarchical, and communalistic one, such as Murray Bookchin. The distinctions between the various positions on this continuum are crucial. It must be emphasized that the mere use of a non-polluting, renewable energy source does not make a given technology an alternative. The very definition of *alternative* technology excludes those technology applications that reflect the highly centralized—"the bigger the better"—grow-or-die ideology of capitalism.

Alternative technology must be understood as a social concept rather than an instrumental technological application of gadgetry to a given problem. Alternative technology reflects a self-conscious notion of the crucial relationship between technics and both the natural and social worlds. At the ISE, while we did develop and demonstrate technologies, our primary concern was always with the social and ecological matrix in which any technology is embedded. Who owns it and who benefits from it? How are decisions made about what technology to develop and deploy, and who controls it? Is it humanly scaled and decentralized? What is the ecological impact?

We saw alternative technology as having great potential for decentralized, humanly scaled applications in the urban setting, and as lending itself to community control and directly democratic forms of decision making, thus providing a material base for the development of a decentralized, directly democratic society. We also understood alternative technology as a way to address growing concerns about pollution, particularly air quality, in the urban environment. Although Bookchin had pointed out the threat of greenhouse gasses as early as 1964, we did not have a sense of urgency concerning climate change. At that time he suggested it might pose a danger in 200 years, but his warnings were ignored, and even, in some cases, ridiculed. In light of today's assessments, we were foolish not to take those concerns more seriously. However, the experience in Loisaida still has relevance to the issue of global warming: Its call for decentralized, democratically controlled, and humanly scaled technology are echoed today in the climate justice movement, which recognizes that industrial scaled and corporate controlled energy production, even if it is based on renewable resources, is still part and parcel of a capitalist society run amok, and, as such, fails to address not only the ecological concerns, but also the questions of social justice, democracy, and equity that were central to the alternative technology movement.

Lower East Side History

New York's Lower East Side is America's portal of immigration and also its archetypal immigrant ghetto. Virtually every major immigrant group that established itself in the United States came through the Lower East Side. The Dutch, who first colonized Manhattan, built their city, New Amsterdam, in the 1620s on the fecund hunting and fishing grounds of the Lenape Indians and extended their Bouries, or farms, into much of the area now known as the Lower East Side. This was not a peaceful process: In 1643 a company of Dutch Militia under the command of Governor Wilhelm Kieft slaughtered a group of forty Indians, mostly women and children, encamped on Corlear's Hook. The Dutch were followed by the British, whose colonial project, resting heavily on the African slave trade, finally collapsed after their defeat in the American Revolution.

The Irish, fleeing the potato famine, were the next group of immigrants to establish themselves on the Lower East Side, mostly in what was known as the Five Points District and around Chatham Square, beginning in the early 19th century. The Irish habitation set the stage for what was to be an on-going way of life on the Lower East Side, the ghettoization of immigrant groups in the physically isolated confines of Corlear's Hook, which jutted out into the East River, cut off from the rest of Manhattan. The isolation, discrimination, poverty, crime, exploitation, and neglect faced by the Irish became a pattern imposed on the many other ethnicities that followed.

Western European Jews, from Germany and Austria, established a strong presence in the 1830s, and other Northern European immigrants flooded the Lower East Side after the failed revolutions of 1848. By the 1860s, over 100,000 residents of German extraction lived around Tomkins Square Park in a neighborhood known as

"Kleindeutschland." Chinatown was established on the Lower East Side beginning in the 1850s, following the depletion of the California gold mines. The 1870s and '80s saw large numbers of Italians, mostly from the South and Sicily, and Eastern European Jews, escaping the pogroms and forced conscription that were their fate in Russia, immigrate to the Lower East Side. At the turn of the century, the Lower East Side had a population density of almost 240,000 people per square mile, greater than the "Black Hole" of Calcutta. These were the people whose plight was documented by the photographer Jacob Riis in his shocking work, *How the Other Half Lives*. The tide of immigration continued until the strict imposition of immigration quotas in 1921.

Puerto Ricans, due to the colonial status of their Island, were excluded from the quotas and established a presence on the Lower East Side beginning in the 1950s. Loisaida is the name they gave to their neighborhood, approximately 30 square blocks, bounded by the East River on the East, Avenue A on the West, 14th Street on the North and Houston Street on the South. By the 21st century, tens of millions of immigrants of various ethnicities had come through the Lower East Side.

The Crises of the 1970s

The 1970s was a period with a growing awareness and concern about energy supplies and energy costs. The United States' dependence on Middle Eastern oil was highlighted by the emergence of OPEC and the Arab oil embargos of 1973 and 1979. Gasoline shortages, rising prices, and long lines at gas stations all contributed to a growing sense of crisis that

President Jimmy Carter called "the moral equivalent of war." Nor was the "energy crisis" the only crisis we were facing.

We were also in the midst of an "urban crisis." The crisis of the cities called into question the very viability of our urban centers. It was characterized by a general trend toward urban decay, finding specific manifestation in fiscal crises, like the one that nearly bankrupted New York City; the breakdown of once identifiable and coherent neighborhoods; the abandonment of whole areas of the City, epitomized by the South Bronx, but also affecting Manhattan neighborhoods like Loisaida; and a widespread erosion of services. All of these trends were symptomatic of a deeply rooted malaise.

The flight of capital from our central cities, exemplified by their rapidly eroding tax bases and the shift of corporate operations to the hinterlands and suburbs, indicated a growing willingness to "write off" our older urban centers. While urban values and urban culture are the predominant forces that have shaped modern American society, the cities themselves were no longer considered essential to our national wellbeing. City after city was being deserted by the middle-class and the cultural elite, and this trend continues today in cities like Detroit and other decaying "rust belt" cities. The festering class and racial tensions that once again flared up in our cities showed that the period of optimism, born of the massive social programs of the 1960s, was over.

Loisaida was the poorest neighborhood in Manhattan. Per Capita income averaged $1,852 per year. Unemployment was estimated at 20%, with a high percentage of the remaining population underemployed (working part time or sporadically). Youth unemployment was close to 40%

and one third of the housing stock consisted of abandoned buildings and rubble-strewn lots owned by the City. The rest of the buildings were rapidly deteriorating: on some blocks the number of abandoned properties was as high as 60%.

The pattern of abandonment began with landlords milking high rents from tenants and refusing to make repairs or deliver services. They also stopped paying taxes to the City. After three years of non-payment the City would move to seize the building, at which point the landlords would bring in arsonists to displace the tenants and burn down the building in order to collect fire insurance. At 519 East 11th Street 14 mysterious fires broke out in a three-month period. By the time the ownership reverted to the City all that were left were burned out brick shells, which often collapsed into a mound of rubble. These derelict five and six story tenement houses and the vacant lots strewn with their rubble were the cityscape of Loisaida.

In an eerie parallel to today, it was ironic that the very forces that contributed to the downfall of our urban centers were proposing the official solutions. When the government bureaucracies, the banks and the large corporations condemned fiscal irresponsibility and informed us that we had to pay the price for our free spending past, failing to mention that the price included exorbitant interest rates and massive public bailouts from which they benefited. We were told that the public must pay the costs and have confidence in its elected leaders to deal with the crisis. The onus for the "urban crisis" had been shifted to those who were its victims, the inner city poor and working people.

The forces that created the crisis stood ready to pick the bones of the ghetto for their own enrichment. The middle class who abandoned the city was ready to return, if the poor could be eliminated. City planners talked about "planned shrinkage" in population that would eliminate the poor by displacing them. The banks, which consistently red-lined areas like Loisaida, refusing to extend credit for low-income housing, stood ready to finance speculators and developers who would revitalize the area to make it attractive to the middle class. Gentrification had already transformed neighborhood after neighborhood in Manhattan, and Loisaida was prime turf for the implementation of those solutions.

The Decentralist Response

There was, however, another response to the crisis of the cities. It was rooted in the decentralist approach to town planning developed by people like Peter Kropotkin in *Fields, Factories, and Workshops*, Ebenezer Howard in *Garden Cities of Tomorrow*, Lewis Mumford in *The Culture of Cities*, Paul and Percival Goodman in *Communitas*, and Murray Bookchin in works like *The Limits of the City* and *From Urbanization to Cities*. It was a response that called for a radical restructuring of cities and a basic redefinition of urban life. It was not a unified movement with a national program or leadership, nor even a strictly political movement. It was, rather, a broad social movement based in neighborhoods and communities involved in transforming the cities at a grassroots level. It was guided by the principle of local self-reliance and concerned with a wide variety of issues related to that principle. The areas that emerged as priorities included community control of schools, health care, law enforcement and governance; urban food production, housing, planning and land use; energy production and conservation, waste treatment, and neighborhood economics.

It was a movement that was influenced by an ecological sensibility, not simply in terms of sensitivity to issues of environmental quality, but in a more profound sense as well. The movement viewed the neighborhood or community as an ecosystem, not merely as a spatial entity. This provided a perspective that emphasized the interrelationship of the various issues outlined above. It urged people to understand the crises that they faced as symptomatic of a deeper social and cultural malaise. It allowed people to develop a holistic vision for the future of their community.

This approach drew on the lessons of natural ecology and worked with ecological principles in developing both its critique of existing forms of urban organization and in the alternatives it put forward. The ecosystem approach stressed the danger inherent in the simplification of an ecosystem, and pointed out that natural systems find unity in diversity: the greater the number of species interacting in an ecosystem the more stable it is. Simplification via the centralization of functions like food and energy production, far removed from the people who rely on them, creates a situation that is not only alienating, but inherently unstable as well. They also understood ecosystems as non-hierarchical: a web of interdependency, not systems based on command and control. Furthermore, they were informed by the scientific insights into the mutualistic nature of natural systems.

The ecological perspective also informed the concern about the environment of the neighborhood. The urban environment of Loisaida consisted of abandoned buildings, garbage filled vacant lots, decaying tenements, deteriorating public parks, streets lined with stripped cars, and soil contaminated with heavy metals and lead paint chips, polluted air and congested streets. Those were the environmental concerns that the movement focused on.

On another level the movement was ecological in that it looked toward newly emerging ecologically sound technologies in areas like energy efficiency, solar energy, wind power, and organic forms of food production to alleviate their environmental problems.

The reintegration of functions like food and energy production into a neighborhood or community was seen as a means of revitalizing the urban environment. The movement for urban alternatives looked toward the introduction of non-polluting, renewable sources of energy as a facet of the reconstitution of the cities. Solar, wind and other alternatives present the possibility of decentralized control and small-scale application. Intensive organic food production techniques were being used in vacant lots and on rooftops to reintroduce the growing of food into the urban economy. All of these techniques were being integrated into plans for neighborhood development that emerged directly from grassroots organizations, rather than from centralized and bureaucratized City or Federal agencies.

While the emphasis was on local control and decentralization, the movement was not isolationist but recognized the need for cooperation and coordination of certain activities, with the insistence that this coordination should be facilitated through the principle of confederation. Rather than beginning with the assumption that centralization was efficient, the movement began with the principle of decentralizing whatever functions could be dealt with in that fashion, and accepted only the degree of central coordination which proved to be necessary. Their vision was the creation of "A world of neighborhoods."

This emphasis on decentralization grew out of a concern for the creation of social forms and institutions which retained a small scale which was accessible to people. A human scale acts as an inhibiting factor to the growth of bureaucracy, and helps to ensure that people can retain direct control over the decisions that affect their lives.

Chino García of CHARAS put it this way: "I myself, my group or my family, is my nucleus. My building is part of it, my block is next. There are family issues, building issues, block issues, there are neighborhood issues, city issues, on to universal issues. Everybody has to look up to that. You can't play games. Things do not just happen, there are always people scheming and manipulating. Therefore every human being must be prepared to deal with this, with issues, with everyday life operation."

"In this society you are unconsciously or consciously a servant for people who manipulate your whole life," García continued. "You can't just sit and allow things to happen. You should take issue with everything, everything that affects you." García's words reflected a growing awareness in Loisaida.

Reconstructing Loisaida

A walk through the streets of Loisaida in 1978 revealed some remarkable things if one knew where to look beyond the garbage-strewn lots and abandoned buildings. Vacant lots on 12th, 11th, 9th, 8th, 3rd Street and Houston Street were producing a bounty of fresh, organically grown tomatoes, lettuce, peppers, squash, and beans. A rooftop on 11th Street had sprouted a windmill and a bank of solar collectors. Numerous buildings, gutted by arsonists and abandoned by greedy landlords, were undergoing tenant directed renovations. An abandoned oil company garage on 8th Street was transformed into a recycling center. A loft on Avenue B served as a center for the construction of portable geodesic domes, which were used as greenhouses on rooftops and in vacant lots. A garbage-filled lot on 9th Street and Avenue C was developed into a cultural plaza for neighborhood residents. Design work had begun on a permanent dome greenhouse intended to house a 2,400 gallon (9,000 liters) pond for raising fish to edible size in an intensive, closed system aquaculture project; fish were also being raised in basements on 11th Street. A youth run community center on Houston Street near the Bowery was retrofit with the first passive solar space heating wall built in New York City. Rooftop gardens were flourishing at various locations around the neighborhood, and rooftop solar greenhouses were under construction.

Alternative technology had come to Loisaida. The projects mentioned above were the result of the work of a loose coalition of grassroots organizations, including the 11th Street Movement, CHARAS, and CUANDO.

The 11th Street Movement was a federation of low-income tenant's cooperatives on East 11th Street between Avenue A and Avenue B. Though mostly Puerto Rican, the movement had a diverse membership including young and old, black and white. In 1973 they were the first group in New York to undertake urban homesteading on a sweat equity basis, which came to be a key concept in the reconstruction of the neighborhood.

The process of Sweat Equity Urban Homesteading began with the formation of a group of homesteaders, initially community activists, who went into the abandoned building as squatters, claiming the space as their own. Often this required confronting the police and resisting eviction by the City. In the early days, repeated efforts were often necessary to lay claim to a building. Since the squatters were poor, unemployed, or underemployed people they lacked the financial resources necessary for traditional approaches to home ownership, where typically banks required a 10% payment of equity in order to get a conventional housing loan. Instead, as the name suggests, they used their own labor, or sweat, as equity. The group then began the physical renovation of the building, which usually required an extended period of time cleaning out mess before the actual construction process could begin. This stage of the process often took up to a year of work.

After the cleaning process was completed, the homesteaders needed to find the materials required for renovation and acquire the skills needed to do the work. They looked first to themselves and other community groups for those resources. They formed an income-limited housing cooperative to negotiate with the City for ownership of the building. At that time, the City saw the buildings as worthless and was anxious to get them back on the tax rolls. Under pressure from the community the City frequently sold the buildings to the homesteaders for a pittance, sometimes as low as $100 per unit.

In the work on 11th Street, local tradesmen and union members helped to train the homesteaders, who then went on to train others. They hustled and scrounged building materials until they were able to secure an interest-free loan from a dairy cooperative in upstate New York, and over a period of six years were able to complete the renovations and provide low-cost, attractive housing for themselves. They would continue to contribute labor each week for the maintenance and management of their building.

Buildings undergoing sweat equity renovation and management are income limited. Homesteaders may sell their apartments, but only for what they have put into them, eliminating profit and effectively removing the property from the real estate market. They can only sell to others who meet low-income guidelines, ensuring a supply of affordable housing for poor people.

By 1978, East 11th Street between Avenues A and B was in the process of rebuilding itself, with two sweat equity low-income tenants cooperatives completed, six other tenement houses under renovation, and an ambitious program of open space reclamation. Their movement grew and, after its initial successes, it would eventually gain national attention. Ultimately over 40 buildings in Loisaida were successfully renovated through the sweat equity process.

519 East 11th Street was the first building in the city to utilize solar energy and wind power. The 11th Street Movement was best known for this solar project, and for their legal battle with the energy company Con Ed over the installation of a rooftop windmill, which resulted in a decision that set the precedent for the purchase and installation of independent power-producing utilities. Today, independent power production constitutes a multi-billion dollar industry.

The 11th Street Movement was also the prime sponsor of El Sol Brillante Community Garden on 12th Street. Under the direction of 11th Street member and ISE alumna Linda Cohen, residents began using organic growing techniques, solar cold frames, and intensive composting and worm production to grow a wide range of crops.

A series of large plywood tanks were constructed in a basement on 11th Street. These tanks provided the basis for experiments in urban aquaculture. Species being cultured included trout, carp, catfish, tilapia, freshwater clams, and crayfish. The tanks were structured after a system used at the ISE, where one tank yielded a harvest of approximately 70 pounds (32 kilos) of fish every six months. The 11th Street Movement was attempting to find ways to integrate the various projects, using wastewater from the fish tanks to fertilize the gardens and garden waste and worms to feed the fish. The hope was to create closed, self-supporting systems.

CHARAS was a small collective which touched the lives of thousands of neighborhood residents. The group still exists today, after over forty years of struggle. In the 1970s its full time members included men and women, mostly young people between 18 and 30. They were local activists who worked on projects involving environmental education and community development. The group was founded after community activists met the designer Buckminster Fuller in the summer of 1967. He introduced them to geodesic domes and they proceeded to build over one hundred domes throughout the city working with school kids, street gangs, garden clubs, and anyone else with the desire. They transformed vacant lots throughout Loisaida into playgrounds, gardens, vest pocket parks and cultural plazas for local artists. CHARAS was active in the area of housing as well, helping to initiate the work on 11th Street, among other projects. Their members included former gang leaders, carpenters, poets, and musicians. They were committed to working with the youth of the neighborhood and showing them alternatives to the street.

Their work centered on La Plaza Cultural Redevelopment Area, situated on the corner of Avenue C and 9th Street, and the adjacent blocks, which was the largest vacant lot on the Lower East Side. This lot, where weeds, garbage, and rubble from collapsed buildings once provided a breeding ground for rats and disease, was transformed into a congenial setting for neighborhood cultural events and festivals, and to this day remains an important community gathering space in Loisaida. Local poets, musicians and dancers performed poetry, Latin music, and folk dances for a cross-section of the community on a regular basis. With its mural depicting the many cultures of the Lower East Side as a centerpiece, La Plaza was an oasis of color in an otherwise bleak cityscape.

It also illustrated the crucial role that arts and culture played for the movements in Loisaida. Local poets developed a school of street poetry, known as Nuyorican (New York Puerto Rican), which spoke about people's lived experience in Loisaida, and dealt with issues like drugs, police brutality, rent strikes, and racism. At the Nuyorican Poets Café on East 6th Street, they invented the form of performance poetry known as the poetry slam. They also developed a vibrant community theater. Bomba and Plena dancers kept Puerto Rican traditional dance and folk music alive, and performed for the community in La Plaza. Local graffiti artists and muralists, working in the tradition of Diego Rivera, presented graphic descriptions of social issues facing the neighborhood by painting on the sides of abandoned buildings.

Music filled the streets of Loisaida, particularly in the warm months when life was lived largely outdoors on the stoops, street corners and open spaces of the neighborhood. The sounds of congeros pulsed up and down the block, salsa bands played at street fairs, in La Plaza, and at local social clubs. The Nueva Canción movement also found expression in Loisaida. A band called Loisaida, founded by CHARAS members Edgardo Rivera and Edwin (Pupa) Santiago, performed music that melded Nueva Canción, Latin rhythms, and hard rock to express a variety of experiences in the neighborhood.

Directly across from La Plaza on 8th Street stood an abandoned oil company garage, squatted and renovated by CHARAS to serve as a neighborhood recycling center. With the closing of the Village Green recycling center on the West Side, CHARAS operated the only recycling program in Lower Manhattan. According to Angelo González, coordinator of the center, it was designed to recycle glass, paper, aluminum and ferrous metals. The recycling center was a major step in the effort to combine ecological concerns and neighborhood restoration.

On Avenue B, at a loft that served as CHARAS headquarters and communal living space, the first of a new generation of lightweight, portable domes was completed. It was built to serve as a portable greenhouse for the Green Guerillas, a citywide group of gardening activists. Luis Lopez, coordinator of the porta-dome project for CHARAS, asserted that domes had a number of other potential uses, including as portable shelters, loft bedrooms and emergency housing.

Lopez and other members also designed a permanent dome to be built in La Plaza, to contain a 2,400-gallon (9,000 liters) tank for raising fish. Utilizing passive solar energy, the dome was designed to produce fish year round with a very low startup cost and minimal energy inputs. That dome was never built in La Plaza, but CHARAS members came to Vermont and, working with a group of our students, constructed it at the ISE center there.

The coordinator of Youth Environmental Action Projects for CHARAS was Luis Guzmán, who later went on to fame as a film actor, but still retains ties to CHARAS and his neighborhood. He noted how "all these projects help people gain a sense of pride in their neighborhood. They help them to see that things here are not hopeless and that if we all work together we can change things. The domes are like a symbol of something new, and it is happening here first."

A concern with environmental action and the use of alternative technology were areas that had been generally associated with the middle class. Popular wisdom had it that low income people were too concerned with daily survival to become involved with the luxuries of environmental and alternative technological concerns. The experience of these groups proved the conventional wisdom wrong. In fact, it was the concern with daily survival that led these groups to begin working with alternative technology. In the words of Edgardo Rivera, they were looking for "survival with style" and alternatives to the arenas of survival traditionally presented to Loisaida residents: survival via welfare, street hustling, menial jobs, or, for a very few, assimilation into the middle class.

Nuyorican poet Miguel Algerian also described the options available for survival in Loisaida: the workaday world at the lowest rung of the economic ladder, and survival via the street. He then mentioned a third option: the establishment of a new set of social economic and political forms that can sustain a people. It is this third option in which CHARAS was engaged. Its members searched for alternatives to the traditional economic options offered by capitalism, alternatives to the individualism and homogenization presented by the mass culture, alternatives to the assimilation of Puerto Rican traditions into main stream America, alternatives to official plans for urban renewal, and alternatives to the sense of powerlessness which permeated their ghetto environment.

CHARAS went on to claim an abandoned elementary school on 9th Street as part of La Plaza Cultural Redevelopment Area. They began squatting the building in 1979 and turned it into El Bohio Cultural and Community Center. There they ran important educational, environmental and cultural programs for 22 years, until they were forcibly evicted by the police acting on the personal orders Rudolph Giuliani, in one of his last official acts as Mayor of New York. Giuliani also tried to reclaim Loisaida's many community gardens in order to auction the lots off to developers. He declared that "The era of socialism on the Lower East Side is over."

Cuando means "when" in Spanish. It was also the acronym for Cultural Understanding and Neighborhood Development Organization, a youth-run organization that offered a variety of educational, recreational, and cultural programs at its center on 2nd Avenue. The group was founded in 1969 by students from the First Street School, a libertarian school founded by Mabel Chrystie, and their members ranged in age from their early teens to their early twenties. When I was first introduced to them and given a tour of their huge abandoned building I felt like I was meeting Peter Pan and the Lost Boys. When they told me of their ambitious plans, I was skeptical of what they could achieve. I was wrong. They spent three years as squatters in the building before community pressure forced the City to offer them a lease.

The reconstruction of the neighborhood in which these groups were involved took a radically different form than the official plans suggested for the neighborhood. The CUANDO experience provides a striking example of the difference. CUANDO was housed in the old Church of All Nations Settlement House on 2nd Avenue at Houston Street, which was part of a twelve square block area proposed as the Cooper Square Redevelopment Project. The group seized the building in 1975 when the church moved out, leaving the youth of the area without a recreational facility. According to CUANDO founder Roberto (Chi Chi) Illa, through continual struggles they were finally able to gain legal recognition of their occupancy in the summer of 1978.

Cooper Square wanted to tear down the CUANDO building and replace it with high-rise, middle-income housing. The youths had different ideas. With the aid of Ted Finch, from the Energy Task Force and under the direction of Fred Cabrera, coordinator of CUANDO's solar project, they completed construction of New York City's first passive solar heat wall to provide space heating for their third floor gymnasium. They installed five window box greenhouses and began developing French intensive gardens on their 5,000 square feet (465 square meters) rooftop. They developed plans for converting a nonfunctional 24,000 gallon (90,000 liters) swimming pool in their basement into a commercial aquaculture facility, and designed an attached solar greenhouse for the south side of their building. Richard Cleghourne, the program coordinator for CUANDO, envisioned the building developing into a center for demonstrating urban alternative technology.

The groups saw alternative technology as having the potential to provide a material base for the development of a cooperatively owned and managed, self-reliant economy for the neighborhood. Coupled with a developing system of community control of neighborhood institutions for education, health care, public safety, sanitation, housing, and planning, this was the basis of the long range, holistic vision that inspired the experiments they undertook.

The projects affected the community on three levels that interacted with and reinforced each other. First, they contributed to meeting the material needs of the people involved and improved the immediate environment of the neighborhood. Concretely, solar energy meant lower bills for oil and electricity. Gardens and aquaculture systems resulted in high quality, healthy food and reduced food costs. The recycling effort helped to alleviate the health hazards presented by garbage in the streets, and provided a small additional income for those involved. Neighborhood children now played in a grassy park rather than a rubble-strewn lot.

In relation to the total population, the number of people affected to varying degrees by alternative technology projects was arguably small. The projects were conceived as pilot and demonstration programs, their impact limited by definition. To meet needs, particularly food and energy needs, in a more significant fashion would have required a massive intensification of the principles demonstrated in the pilot projects.

Secondly, the alternative technology projects provided a valuable focus for community organizing. The groups were remarkably successful in involving neighborhood young people in their work. They managed to draw youth off the street and in some cases even recruited participants from neighborhood gangs. The energies of the street, which claimed so many of Loisaida's youth, were drawn upon and channeled into productive directions.

The gardening projects in particular drew participation from a broad cross-section of the community. Many of the older gardeners brought experience from years of gardening on the Island of Puerto Rico. The gardens, housing cooperatives, and recycling efforts were all arenas in which the participants developed the skills of self-management necessary for community control.

Participatory Politics

The organizational forms which emerged were truly grassroots and participatory. Each organization functioned as an autonomous group and each had a particular structure, but they all reflected a common concern with ensuring that all of those involved in a particular project participated in making the decisions that affected that project. Emphasis was placed on teaching rather than telling participants how to work together. Learning by doing was the rule of thumb, and youth were given positions of responsibility to help develop their leadership skills. Leadership itself was defined in non-hierarchical terms. People lead by example and by virtue of their experience. Leadership shifted from individual to individual in relation to the specific activity. The processes of both decision-making and physical work were seen as inseparable from, and as equally important as, the end result.

Leadership in CHARAS was situational, shifting from task to task, with everyone in the organization at some point providing leadership in one activity or another, often defying stereotypes, with women taking on a variety of leadership roles, including in traditionally male arenas like construction. When working on projects, CHARAS always tried to involve the broader community. As Chino García put it: "We try to make it, as much as we can, a collective effort. It is not easy. A lot of people don't know how to work with a collective structure. A lot of people want leadership, we have that trouble. They feel that they are useless without it. They want some central body. They're used to dictatorship, not their own plans and preparations. We try to teach them to be more independent of a central body, more independent as a team."

That "people should work together collectively," was the explicit ideal. García further described the process: "We try to make decisions as a group. Things are written by the group and signed 'collectively' rather than 'respectfully.' It means the group decided. We do not use names like 'Director,' we are not traditional leaders; we call ourselves co-coordinators of what has to be done." The whole point being that CHARAS "try to get people to the point where they can be their own bosses; develop their skills and break out of that whole leader/led mindset," García concluded.

This process of personal empowerment was reflected in the integration of new members into the group. Leadership took on an educational form, teaching people to become leaders themselves by empowering individuals to become an effective part of a collective decision making process. CHARAS had a mechanism known as the Yucca system. The principle at work, according to Angelo González, was "Each one teach one."

This practical learning experience was powerful. "I felt close to my people. I wanted to do something, about the neighborhood," said Luis Guzmán, describing his experience as a seventeen-year-old. "When I was in high school I was part of a study group of students and we would discuss things, like how the economic system works, why we have poor people, really breaking it down, you know, how the system works, different forms of government. My mind was developing, questioning lots of things." Guzmán did organizing for the United Farm Workers when he met Chino García, who invited him over to CHARAS. "I started getting more involved, going to meetings, getting involved with committees, and learning a lot about community politics, being asked to speak about the community and my feelings." In the process, "I opened up to a lot of ideas, learned to make judgments, say yes or no; to develop a sense of myself, and a commitment to the movement and my people; to understand the system, come up with alternatives and think positive." Participation affected everything, he explained: "It's like being a warrior, you have to learn everything out there and change yourself, you can't learn it all from books."

If politics is defined in its most basic sense as the way people relate to each other and make decisions that govern their lives, then the movement in Loisaida must be understood as intensely political. But not so if politics is defined in its narrow, more generally accepted sense as the parliamentarian or sectarian exercise of political power. The groups did not conform to a particular political ideology, doctrine, or dogma. However their practice was informed by a set of principles.

Edgardo Rivera explained it this way, "A different kind of politics is emerging. A state of change is happening. Rather than push one model or one program on people you have to be participatory and give support to things that are beneficial to the people and the environment of the neighborhood." In reference to CHARAS he said, "Everyone is an individual with their personal beliefs, but as an organization CHARAS does not identify itself with any system, party, or political organization. It is not separatist politics; it is a matter of direction." The basic idea was that the community should address its own needs. "We are aiming for the area to define its own future," said Rivera. "As people keep learning they realize that there is a lot they can do themselves to make things better." The political implications were obvious: "You suddenly realize that nobody should plan for anybody else," Rivera explained. "We meet our own needs. The community meetings serve that purpose."

The major emphasis of CHARAS was exemplary action and praxis. In the words of Victor Sanchez, a prison organizer and former member of CHARAS, "The concept is based on the practice of self-reliance and self-determination. We do not deal with ideology or false pride. We are about work." To be sure, "When you talk about community development, in the long run you are talking about controlling the police, the schools, everything," Sanchez admitted. "We are aware of the fact that we live in a country full of contradictions; we don't need any more contradictions among ourselves. So we try to set an example of how things can be done."

"The practice centers on everyday life," Sanchez explained. "Did you eat today? Do you have heat? We are open." Indeed, "we have been accused of being liberal, too open, too vulnerable. But it is not liberalism," he insisted: "we just don't want our organization to be used as a platform for someone's ideology." Their rejection of sectarian ideology should not be misinterpreted as anti-intellectualism or ignorance, rather it was a conscious choice to develop a politics based in direct action and a reconstructive vision, and a recognition of the inadequacies of sectarian political theory in dealing with the particulars of their situation.

The organizations involved were part of a larger network of Lower East Side groups involved in housing, health care, educational and cultural issues. For several years these groups assembled at quarterly Loisaida town meetings to make plans, discuss the problems and celebrate the triumphs of their neighborhood. These town meetings, attended by individual citizens and representatives of over one hundred community organizations, were initiated by the Institute of Cultural Affairs, a Chicago-based group devoted to grassroots community empowerment and reconstruction, rooted in a utopian, communal, Christian tradition. While overt religiosity was rejected by most of the groups and individuals who participated in the town meetings, the forum itself proved to be extremely valuable as a way to make decisions about neighborhood priorities, assign responsibility for specific projects, and coordinate activities between groups.

At the town meetings the community was divided up, block by block, and detailed plans were blueprinted for the redevelopment of each abandoned building and vacant lot, with responsibility for each project assigned to a specific neighborhood group. A comprehensive plan for the neighborhood resulted.

Over 300 individuals attended a typical town meeting. Decisions were made using direct democracy, and the decisions affected a group of approximately 3,000 people actively engaged in the process of community reconstruction in Loisaida, about 10% of the total population of the neighborhood. Given that a large number of neighborhood residents were children and another large percentage of the population were involved with crime, drugs, and other activities that made their participation unlikely, 3,000 people constituted a significant block of Loisaida's citizenry. The groups also produced a magazine focused on community issues, *The Quality of Life in Loisaida*.

Mutual Aid

Another level on which the projects affected the neighborhood was more long term. While the projects that I have described were experiments and pilot projects they were all seen as having a potentially transformative impact on Loisaida. The economic development of the area through alternative technology meant not only the physical reconstruction of the neighborhood, but the creation of jobs, job training and new sources of income as well. Such opportunities were desperately needed in Loisaida, where estimates of unemployment among youth ran as high as 40%. Job training was provided to people in the rapidly emerging fields related to alternative technologies like solar energy and retrofitting buildings for energy efficiency. Jobs for those trained could have been developed in the neighborhood itself where about 70% of the housing stock was abandoned or dilapidated.

The groups began to create small-scale cooperative businesses to put their skills to use. CHARAS began building portable domes. CUANDO constructed window box greenhouses that they hoped to market. Plans were made for the expansion of the recycling center to full resource recovery from raw garbage. The members of CUANDO designed an attached greenhouse for their 2nd Avenue center to supply ornamental plants for neighborhood shops in addition to raising vegetables. The 11th Street Movement constructed two rooftop greenhouses for food production. A carpentry cooperative and a tool lending library were developed on 11th Street, as was a solar installation cooperative. Sweat equity buildings throughout the neighborhood formed a fuel oil purchasing cooperative, and the community started both a food cooperative, and a community credit union.

The development and survival of the projects in Loisaida rested on an economic base rooted in the tradition of mutual aid. It drew on Puerto Rican communal traditions, and a sense of mutualism often found in immigrant communities, with mechanisms like hometown clubs, extended family networks and street cliques providing support and sharing resources. The motto of CHARAS was "Doing more with less." As Chino García described it, "It means to take a dollar and stretch it, by not being individualists and one person or group hog it all."

In CHARAS people shared money as it became available; reciprocity was the principle at work. Individual needs were taken into account; a father of two children would receive more than a single person. The rule was "from each according to his or her ability, to each according to his or her need." Edgardo Rivera said, "Sometimes we get paid, sometimes we don't. Sometimes someone may have an outside job, or unemployment. We share, we stay open, people are happy, and they survive. Sometimes it is hard to believe that no one has any money."

Funding for the projects has come from a variety of sources: community churches, private foundations, public grants, and low interest loans. After the work was already established, the three groups received $96,000 from the National Center for Appropriate Technology (NCAT), an independent organization funded by the federal Community Services Administration to finance experiments in alternative technology for low-income people. NCAT funded numerous projects around the country, though most focused on the application of alternative technology in rural situations. The projects in Loisaida were the first attempt at a concerted application of alternative technology in the urban environment. Hiram Shaw, the acting Director of NCAT, believed that "If it can work in New York, it can work anywhere."

The groundwork for the projects was laid over a period of several years. Technical assistance through the planning and design phases was provided by a number of groups and individuals, including Buckminster Fuller, the Energy Task Force, Adopt-a-Building, the Urban Homestead Assistance Board, the Green Guerrillas, landscape architect Robert Nichols, and the Institute for Social Ecology. This collaboration between radical environmentalists and the low-income Puerto Rican community of Loisaida was unprecedented. The cooperation provided a strong argument against those who claimed that environmental issues were irrelevant to inner city people.

It is important to note that while outside assistance was instrumental in making the projects a reality, the primary impetus rested within the Loisaida community. Chino García noted that "In the '60s the anti-poverty program came into the neighborhood with millions of dollars, and the government had all these programs that were going to help us out and save the Lower East Side. Those programs were supposed to be controlled by the people, but they never really were. So those millions of dollars were spent and nothing really changed, in fact things got worse. Some people got the idea that the government would provide for them. But some of us came to understand that we had to do for ourselves if we really wanted to control what happens in our neighborhood. That's what the environmental projects are about. We do for ourselves, we use whatever resources we have available in the community ('doing more with less') and after we have gone as far as we can go we look to the outside for some help. We welcome assistance from the outside, but they have to understand that the community will make the decisions about what goes on and the community will own and control whatever we build up."

This emphasis on grassroots control and decision-making was crucial to the success of the projects. It enabled alternative technology to gain a foothold in this neighborhood where other efforts to introduce alternative technology to the inner city, like the community technology experiments in Washington, D.C., which Karl Hess wrote about in his book *Community Technology*, had failed. These were not groups of middle class people bringing the blessings of alternative technology to the poor. Rather, the efforts were an expression of the people of the neighborhood demanding access to the tools that could enable them to reconstruct their own neighborhood. In the words of Angelo González of CHARAS, "It is the human energy, not the solar energy that will really make the difference."

Reflections on Gentrification

While the projects were but a tiny fragment of the work that needed to be done if Loisaida was to be turned around from its state of decay, they represented an important first step. The use of forms of neighborhood organization for which the technologies can provide a material base had the potential to transform the Lower East Side. There was, of course, no guarantee that such a transformation would occur. The projects were underfinanced, understaffed, and frustrated by the constant bureaucratic entanglements involved in any community work. But given the technological and more importantly human energies involved, there was great hope for "un milagro de Loisaida," a miracle of the Lower East Side. That miracle, the transformation and reconstruction of America's archetypal immigrant ghetto, had important implications for all of our decaying cities, and for the redefinition of an urban lifestyle for all of our citizens.

Clearly, the technologies were not a panacea. In fact, technology in and of itself can offer no solution to what are essentially social problems. But they did hold the potential to support the emerging cultural movement in Loisaida in significant ways. I wish I could point to Loisaida today as a model for a an ecological, self-reliant, directly-democratic neighborhood built on the rubble of a collapsed capitalist society, but the reality is that the larger economic and political forces of the city and nation-state conspired to prevent the developments described above from reaching their full potential. We discovered that, to paraphrase Lenin, you cannot build ecotopia in one neighborhood. From the early 1980s, the movement was forced to turn its attention to the battle against gentrification.

As the US economy recovered from the recession of the early 1980s and entered the era of Ronald Reagan, Loisaida was targeted for "development." Just a twenty minute walk from Wall Street, the vacant lots and abandoned buildings were seen as ripe for picking by real estate developers, who rechristened the neighborhood "alphabet city." Ironically, a major factor that made the neighborhood so attractive was the revitalization of the community through the efforts of the grassroots. Vacant lots were now community gardens, abandoned houses were being rehabbed, and a vibrant New York Puerto Rican culture had emerged. Artists, punk rockers, and students seeking low rents were moving east of Avenue A, and bringing clubs, restaurants and shops with them. A new "hip" neighborhood was taking shape, and real estate was cheap. Speculators started moving in.

The building next to the CHARAS loft on Avenue B changed hands three times in an eighteen month period, first for $12,000, then for $36,000 and finally for $320,000, without any work or renovation being done. The City changed its policy and instead of negotiating with community groups for ownership of abandoned properties, all City owned buildings and lots were put on the auction block.

A huge struggle was waged when the Giuliani administration decided to evict the community gardens and auction off the lots on which they were built. Squatters were targeted for eviction and long-standing community projects were under assault. The jiu jitsu of the real estate market forced the community of Loisaida to fight a holding action, which resulted in numerous confrontations with the police and the New York City Housing Authority.

The gentrification of the neighborhood moved into high gear during the 1980s. The active displacement of low income residents increased, with landlords using arson, harassment, and intimidation to force out renters, abetted by the City's efforts to build middle income housing that would have excluded most of the poor and working people of Loisaida. The City also tried to divide various constituencies in the neighborhood; they proposed middle income artists housing be built on the site of La Plaza Cultural, a move that was successfully resisted by CHARAS and other community groups, including artists groups.

In the 1990s, the City renovated Tomkins Square Park in the heart of Loisaida and used the opportunity to tear down the amphitheater there, which had served as an important center for cultural and political gatherings, and to push the homeless population, which had been a strong presence in the park, out of the neighborhood in order to "sanitize" it for the more middle class residents starting to move east of Avenue A. In 1990 a massive riot began in the park and roiled into the surrounding blocks as a protest against these actions.

The community groups held a series of protests and direct actions to try to stem the tide of displacement; they fought back in every way imaginable. They were forced to abandon their ambitious plans for reconstructing their neighborhood and put all of their energy into fighting gentrification. The shifting population dynamics insured the election of a city council member who was a proponent of gentrification, and the real estate interests, arguably the most powerful force in New York politics, stepped up the pressure on the city for market sales of city owned properties. By the mid 1990s, gentrification of the Lower East Side was a fait accompli. Some of the community groups were able to hold on to what they had built up; Sweat equity groups who had negotiated legal title to their buildings were able to keep them. The actress Bette Midler gave millions of dollars so that some community gardens were purchased from the city and placed in a public trust, after years of protest and resistance. However, many more groups lost their hard-earned projects. After 22 years of operation, CHARAS was evicted from El Bohio, based in the old public school on 9th Street, and they also lost their recycling center on 8th Street. CUANDO was evicted, their property sold, and ultimately torn down. One of the most promising grassroots efforts at neighborhood reconstruction ever attempted was crushed under the weight of the real estate market.

In retrospect it is clear that the movement made some strategic mistakes. When the neighborhood was redlined by the banks and the abandoned properties were considered worthless by the City, the grassroots groups should have organized to ensure a comprehensive approach to community ownership and control of those properties, rather than the piecemeal approach that emerged. We should have had the foresight to realize that, given the pattern that had emerged in so many Manhattan neighborhoods before (like Greenwich Village, SoHo and Tribeca), gentrification posed a real threat, something that was hard to believe walking through the mostly abandoned neighborhood of the 1970s.

The City could have been pressured to guarantee community access as a first priority for City owned properties. This approach was used by the Dudley Street Neighborhood Initiative in Boston and they were able to secure their part of the Roxbury neighborhood for community ownership and community based development efforts. There was a City wide coalition of grassroots groups that included the South Bronx People's Development Organization, the Banana Kelly Block Association, the Brooklyn based National Council of Neighborhood Women, and numerous other grassroots organizations dealing with housing and open space issues, which could have mobilized to put more pressure on the Department of Housing Preservation and Development to insure community ownership and provide more public spending for Sweat Equity Urban Homesteaders, a position which would have garnered broad public support since Sweat Equity produced low income housing at approximately one fourth of the cost of building traditional public housing.

The movement also failed to fully develop the potential of the town meetings as a counterpower to the City government, a strategy later developed by Murray Bookchin in his concept of libertarian municipalism. As the pressure of gentrification increased the town meetings fell by the wayside, replaced, in part, by the democratization of the Community Planning Board, which now consists of elected, rather than appointed, representatives. Representative democracy, however, is not a replacement for the direct democracy practiced in the town meeting forum, and this, I believe, led to a growing disempowerment of residents.

An approach which combined protest and direct action, the two primary methods used by the movement, with the genuinely political dimension expressed through the town meetings could have had a powerful impact and set the stage for the creation of real community power. In addition to reinforcing the democratic inclination of the people in the neighborhood, and providing them with education and experience in the exercise of direct democratic decision-making, such a strategy could conceivably have presented a powerful counter-force to the real estate developers. And it could have been further advanced to challenge the very structures of decision-making that govern the City, ultimately forcing a change of charter and a redefinition of governance that would have allowed for the full realization of their vision of "a world of neighborhoods."

From a distance of almost forty years it is easy to see the shortcomings of what we attempted. However, given the urgency of the crises we currently face, the growing dependence of the planet on dwindling supplies of fossil fuels, the need to immediately deal with climate change, and the imperative to address all of these crises in a fashion that emphasizes freedom and equity, the lessons of Loisaida loom large, both as an inspiration and as a cautionary tale.

THE UTOPIAN IMPULSE

The ecosphere is threatened to a degree unprecedented in humanity's tenure on the planet. The rupture with the natural world is symptomatic of and a causal factor in the breakdown of social relations. The consciousness of exploitation and domination extends to both people and nature and given their concurrent evolution it is unlikely that one will be eliminated exclusive of the other.

The ecology movement, at least in its most conscious manifestations, has recognized the need for a reconstructive vision that acknowledges the primary importance of these interrelations. The radical ecology movement rejects simple technical fixes as the solution to ecological problems that have their roots deeply embedded in the culture. The movement has stressed the need for a holistic approach to ecological problems and further, has suggested that basic changes in the ethos of the culture and the structure of its institutions are necessary if we are to ever achieve a truly ecological society.

Radical ecologists are attempting to create a theory and practice for such an ecological society: a reconstructive vision that they can begin to actualize in the here and now. In the creation of their reconstructive praxis they draw inspiration from many sources, including the scientific discipline of ecology, the traditional cultures of Native American peoples, and the spiritual paths of the East.

There is another tradition that informs their vision as well though unfortunately it remains largely unknown, ignored, misunderstood, or unacknowledged, even by the movement itself. It is the utopian tradition.

The Utopian Tradition

While using a different language and set of references, the utopian tradition in many ways parallels the concerns of the radical ecology movement. There is much in the history and theory of utopia that can help illuminate critical problems in social ecology.

What follows are reflections on that utopian tradition, a typological analysis which differentiates various strains in the tradition, and an analysis of those aspects of the tradition most relevant to the emerging praxis of the radical ecology movement.

Throughout the whole of history there have been attempts to transform the given social conditions in basic ways, to visualize and to actualize a society more harmonious, fulfilling and clearly close to ideal than the one given. These attempts have taken a variety of forms ranging from the purely philosophical and conceptual to the reconstructive and revolutionary. In a broad sense, these efforts can be understood as part of the utopian impulse.

Utopia is a term coined by Sir Thomas More in 1515. He traces the root to two Greek words: *outopia*, translated as no place, and *eutopia*, the good place. The word has acquired, since Frederick Engles' critique of "utopian" socialism in *Anti-Duhring*, the negative connotation of *outopia*—cloud cuckoo land. For our purposes, the term must be understood in a more neutral way: as a description of an approach to social reconstruction oriented toward the creation of an "ideal" society.

The utopian impulse is a response to existing social conditions and an attempt to transcend or transform those conditions to achieve an ideal. It always contains two interrelated elements: a critique of existing conditions and a vision or reconstructive program for a new society. Utopias usually arise during periods of social upheaval, when the old ways of a society are being questioned by new developments. Thus, Plato's *Republic* emerged in Athens after the victory of Sparta in the Peloponnesian Wars, More's *Utopia* emerged during the Age of Discovery, and the industrial revolution gave birth to numerous utopian experiments.

While these utopias and countless others are all distinct in a programmatic sense they share certain structural elements.

The combination of critique and reconstructive vision has already been noted. They also share a holistic perspective, focusing on the reformation of society as a whole rather than the simple reform of specific social institutions. They tend to choose a humanly scaled community as their locus of action and elaborate their transformative vision within that context.

Utopias often display an orientation toward "happiness," defined in terms of material plenty—as communal property—and "justice," a concept defined in widely divergent ways. They frequently emphasize equality between men and women, and an integration of town and country. The themes of balance and harmony resonate throughout utopia.

Utopias develop their vision either by drawing on residual traditional elements or historic tendencies of a society that are seen as positive and elaborating and supporting those elements—as Plato took inspiration from aspects of Greek tradition—or by drawing upon and elaborating new developments, often scientific or technological, that seem to hold promise—as Francis Bacon did in his *New Atlantis*.

The impulse toward utopia has persisted over millennia. Paul Radin suggests that even primitive hunters and gatherers harkened toward utopia, as reflected in their dream/myths of a past Golden Age that would return in the near future. We see a certain continuity of utopian thought from the philosophical writings of Plato through the Christian myths about the Garden of Eden and eschatology.

In more recent times, utopia has shifted from the religious to the secular arena. From the Enlightenment onward, utopia began taking a more explicitly social form. Here too though, we must distinguish between the utopias of intellect and attempts to actualize utopia through communalistic or revolutionary experiments.

In examining the broad historic tradition that comprises the utopian impulse we can develop general categories of utopias that display similar characteristics. At one end of the continuum, the literary and philosophical utopias present a theoretical "blueprint" for a perfect society, while on the other end, utopian social theories, experiments and movements make concrete attempts to bring about "utopia."

These two approaches to utopia are described by Lewis Mumford in *The Story of Utopias*: "One of these functions is escape or compensation; it seeks an immediate release from the difficulties or frustrations of our lot. The other attempts to provide a condition for our release in the future." Mumford called these "Utopias of escape" and "Utopias of reconstruction," respectively: "The first leaves the external world the way it is; the second seeks to change it so that one may have intercourse with it on one's own terms. In one we build impossible castles in the air; in the other we consult a surveyor and an architect and a mason and proceed to build a house which meets our essential needs; as well as houses built of stone and mortar are capable of meeting them."

Philosophical and literary utopias are the work of individuals and as such tend to reflect their creators' likes and dislikes. These idiosyncratic approaches have given rise to the cliché that "One man's utopia is another man's hell." While the philosophical utopias address important social problems they tend to generate "solutions" that take the form of mechanistic plans requiring an authoritarian social structure for enforcement. They are usually hierarchical, dogmatic, static societies. This rationalization of society and the concurrent rigidifying of social hierarchies was described by Karl Popper and brilliantly explored in Stanley Diamond's critique of Plato's *Republic*—the archetypal literary utopia.

Utopian Social Movements

Reconstructive utopian social movements approach the problem of creating a new social order in a more organic fashion. The emphasis at the outer edge of the continuum is on utopian process, with the actual reconstructive details of the "new society" left to the participants' determination. At this end of the continuum we can place the various "people's utopias" which have a long history suggested by the early slave revolts, early Christian Gnostic communities, and the heretic communities seen as part of the Gnostic or Anabaptist tradition, like the Cathars in France, the Paterini and Lombardi in Italy, the Brotherhood of Free Spirits, the True Levelers and Diggers during the English Revolution, the revolt of Thomas Munster and other movements of the Reformation, peasant revolts, the Paris Commune, and in the late nineteenth and twentieth centuries anarchist praxis in Russia, Spain, and elsewhere.

These are the more libertarian forms of utopia, to varying degrees participatory, democratic and non-hierarchical, and all dynamic and transformative in their approach.

In Mumford's words: "The Utopia of reconstruction is what its name implies: A vision of a reconstituted environment which is better adapted to the nature and aims of the human beings who dwell within it than the actual one; and not merely better adapted to their actual nature, but better fitted to their possible development." Furthermore, "By a reconstructed environment I do not mean merely a physical thing. I mean in addition a new set of habits, a fresh scale of values, a different net of relationships and institutions."

At a variety of points between the extremes, we can place the ideal constitutions, planned communities, intentional communities, communes, and revolutionary movements. They conform to a general definition of utopia that includes the combination of critique and reconstructive program—a holistic vision of the new society that insists on the integration of the various psychological, social, economic, political, and spiritual aspects of society.

The tradition of the reconstructive "people's utopias" is an old one, predating the literary and philosophical. It is in all probability a tendency that predates written history. "People's utopias" have been efforts on the part of groups of people to actualize their utopia rather than to relegate it to a lost paradise or to defer it until death. They have been concerned with a total restructuring of society from the bottom up. These efforts have taken the form of attempts to institute the new social order either through the creation of separatist intentional communities or through active revolutionary opposition to the old order.

The communitarian efforts of the classic "utopians"— Saint-Simon, Fourier, and Robert Owen—were an outgrowth of the idiosyncratic "systems" usually associated with the literary tradition. Yet they did attempt to bring their utopias into being and in so doing laid the foundations for modern socialist thought, which can itself be understood as a further expression of utopia. On the other end of the continuum of "people's utopias" stand the revolutionary anarchist movements of the nineteenth and twentieth centuries.

Utopianism and Socialism

One way of defining utopian social movement in the nineteenth century is by examining the distinction between these movements and the "scientific socialism" of their chief critics, Marx and Engels. The Marxist critique of utopian socialism is most clearly expressed by Engels in *Anti-Duhring*. He acknowledges the contributions made by Fourier, Saint-Simon, and Owen toward the formulation of the basic ideas of socialism. In Saint-Simon, Engels explains, "we find a comprehensive breadth of view, by virtue of which almost all the ideas of later socialists, that are not purely economic, are found in him in embryo." Of the utopians in general he states, "We delight in the stupendously grand thought and germs of thought that everywhere break out through their phantastic covering."

It is the "phantastic covering" of Saint-Simon's system of which Engels was critical. He argued that Saint-Simon's utopia, a unification of science and industry in a "New Christianity" in which the bourgeois are transferred into public servants by the spirit of reason and cooperation, was an expression of a period when industrial capitalism and its ensuing class antagonisms were still in an undeveloped state. Though he recognized an embryonic class-consciousness in Saint-Simon's overriding concern for "the class that is the most numerous and most poor," ultimately Saint-Simon is seen to be dominated by the historical situation that stimulated his theory: "To the crude conditions of capitalist production and the crude class conditions corresponded crude theories."

Fourier is praised by Engels for his astute and biting criticism of French society. However, in Engels' words, "Fourier is at his greatest in his conception of the history of society. He divides its whole course, thus far, into four stages of evolution—savagery, barbarism, the patriarchate and civilization." Engels sees in Fourier's historical ideas an application of dialectics analogous to Kant's use of the method in natural science. Yet, Fourier, despite his brilliant insights into the workings of society and history, projected a complete system as the solution to France's social problems. Engels said, "These new social systems were foredoomed as Utopian; the more completely they were worked out in detail the more they could not avoid drifting off into pure phantasies."

Yet, by dismissing Fourier's "phantasies" Engels and others dismissed the most prescient and provocative aspects of Fourier's thought: his emphasis on the emotional content of life in his utopia, a whole psychodynamic dimension displaying a set of concerns with the nonmaterial quality of everyday life. Unfortunately, this did not reemerge as a major theme in socially reconstructive thought until the 1960s, when it was advanced by theorists such as Herbert Marcuse and Norman O. Brown.

The idiosyncratic element in these utopian systems was, in Engels' view, inevitable. As with the literary and philosophical utopias, they were the works of individual thinkers who saw the new society arising out of reason and self-conscious activity, divorced from a specific historical period and level of economic development. They were an expression of the likes and dislikes of their creators, conditioned by their subjective views and expressing their own absolute truths. Unfortunately, in his search for "science" and in his insistence on a narrowly defined class analysis, Engels rejects some of the more profound aspects of the French utopian tradition.

Robert Owen was a formulator of systems as well, but the industrial capitalism of nineteenth-century England, where Owen put his theories into practice, was significantly more developed than in France. Owen, who began his career as a social reformer from the unlikely position of factory manager, gradually came to believe that socialism was the only means of guaranteeing justice to the working class he saw battered and degraded by the new system of production. Owen made the transition from philanthropist to socialist upon his realization that "the newly created gigantic productive forces, hitherto used only to enrich individuals and to enslave the masses, offered the foundations for a reconstruction of society; they were destined, as the common property of all, to be worked for the common good of all." He saw private property, religion, and the present form of marriage as the obstacles to the institution of his ideal society. While his attempt to actualize his ideal in the form of a communist community in Indiana met with failure, he was a major influence on the British working class. Owen's communism, grounded in the materialist view that people were a product of their heredity, but moreover their environment, was still an appeal to reason. Rather than looking to the proletariat to emancipate themselves, he demonstrated the logic of his system and hoped to convince the bourgeoisie through that logic.

This brings us to another crucial point in Engels' critique of the utopians. He states that despite a genuine concern for the working class, "one thing is common to all three. Not one of them appears as a representative of the interests of that proletariat, which historical development had in the meantime produced." Here Engels is referring to the failure of Saint-Simon, Fourier and Owen to represent the interests of the proletariat exclusively, based on their lack of perception of what he saw as the deep, irreparable chasm which developed between bourgeois and proletariat under the impetus of industrial capitalism. There can be no doubt that all three were concerned with the plight of the working class but they did not envision the new society born of a confrontation between classes over control of the means of production. Theirs was not a truly revolutionary socialism; they still believed in the ideal of reason, which lay at the root of the bourgeois revolutions, and in the ability of reason to bring about the new social order. The essence of Engels' critique of the utopians lies not with their formulation of the basic ideals of socialist theories, but with their lack of understanding of the process by which the new society may be brought into being and their idiosyncratic projections of what form the new society will take.

Marxism, Anarchism, and the State

After the classic utopians, socialism began to take on an identity as a revolutionary movement, first in France, later in other European nations. This development followed two distinct paths, the "scientific" socialism of Marx and Engels, and a continued "utopianism" best presented by the anarchists Proudhon, Bakunin and Kropotkin. Both positions were influential among the emerging workers' movement; Marx's influence was strongest in Germany and England where an industrial proletariat had developed and, according to Marx's theory, the material conditions were sufficiently evolved to allow for the development of socialism. The anarchists' theories were embraced by workers' movements in France, Italy, Switzerland and Spain, where the craft tradition of the small workshop and individual producer had not entirely given way to the factory system necessary for the creation of a true industrial proletariat.

The Marxists and anarchists were the two major forces in the newly formed International Working Men's Association, the First International. Though doctrinal differences had surfaced before the formation of that organization—most notably in the dispute between Marx and Proudhon, sparked in part by Proudhon's refusal to collaborate with Marx—it was in the First International that the issues that divided the Marxist "scientific" socialists and anarchist "utopians" clearly surfaced.

The differences revolved around three interrelated questions concerning class analysis, organizational form, and the role of the state.

Though the anarchists recognized a severe class antagonism and had discarded the classic utopian's view that the bourgeois would reform themselves, they did not accept Marx's notion that the only truly revolutionary class was an industrial proletariat, organized and disciplined by the factory system. They posited the concept of revolutionary activity arising from a multiplicity of classes: workers, to be sure, but also peasants, déclassé intellectuals and students, and even the *sans-culottes*, that lumpen element for which Marx had nothing but contempt. The Marxists criticized this position as petit bourgeois. Indeed, in Proudhon we do see a naïve belief in the ability of the workers to create the new society without a direct confrontation with the owners, but Bakunin and Kropotkin both clearly express a belief in class struggle as the means of carrying out the "social revolution." The dispute lies then not with the concept of class struggle, but with the composition of the classes that make the revolution.

The second major dispute was based on two very different concepts for organizing the socialist movement. Marx saw the need for a rigid, disciplined, centralized party organization that would take as its model that most efficient form of organization yet devised: the factory system. Workers, organized and disciplined by the industrial processes, would find the embryo of the new society within the sweatshop of the old and use any means possible, including parliamentary activity, to end its exploitation. The anarchists were highly critical of this approach. They saw it as a repetition of the bourgeois pattern in the sense that it was hierarchical, authoritarian and stifling to people's individual initiative. They believed that this approach, though it might bring economic justice, would perpetuate the larger structures of bourgeois society. They were not simply concerned with ending exploitation, an essentially economic concept, but with ending domination as well, a broader social concern. They opted for an organizational model that was decentralized, egalitarian, anti-authoritarian and committed to a strategy of direct action. The anarchists believed that the means and ends of their movement could not be separated: that the form of organization for building the new society must be congruent with the forms they wished to create in that new society.

This dispute over organizational forms is directly connected to the third major area of disagreement: the role of the state. Marx called for the creation of a "dictatorship of the proletariat" that would seize state power, and through a transitional period, pave the way for the "withering away of the state." The anarchists were convinced that rather than withering away, such a state would make its highest priority its own perpetuation. They proposed the dissolution of the state per se, and its replacement by a decentralized federation of autonomous production units and communities, which under direct self-management would coordinate the economic and social life of what was formerly the state.

Communities, Associations, and Communes

With *communist* anarchists like Bakunin and Kropotkin, we see a new definition of utopia emerge. They were not concerned with blueprinting the ideal society for inherent in their approach was an aversion to "systems" and preconceived utopias. Rather they tried to develop a process whereby a multiplicity of new societies could form themselves. They had a strong belief in cultural diversity as a value to be encouraged for its own sake. They recognized in the vestiges of authentic community life that survived the state, as well as the new organizations created by the workers, the embryo of the new society. They visualized communism developing in accordance with the specific cultural tradition of each community, and each community, though participating in a regional and national economy, retaining a distinct cultural identity and the greatest degree of autonomy possible, without sacrificing that degree of coordination necessary to insure the smooth functioning of an industrial society. They saw the creation of a network of such self-managed communities, social and economic units as a substitute for the state.

The anarchist vision of the new society took much of its inspiration from what they saw as the authentic social life and culture of the people. They envisioned personal responsibility and self-conscious ethical behavior taking the place of law. They called for the creation of "people's assemblies" as the basic unit of governance. Kropotkin specifically offers the *folkmoot* of the Medieval commune; the Russian *mir*, or peasant village commune; and the cantonal structures of Switzerland as possible models. The anarchists developed concepts of leadership that were substantially different from those which ruled bourgeois society. Their ideal was much closer to communal and traditional leadership roles, with leaders emerging in specific situations *because of* specific skills, and with responsibility and decision making ultimately lying with the collectivity. The anarchists' brand of communism was close to the communal economic base characteristic of pre-state peoples. They envisioned the creation of self-reliant communities which integrated industry and agriculture, town and country, and work and play. They projected the collectivization of the means of production under the direct control of the workers and peasants, not mediated by the state—as it is under a policy of nationalization—and coordinated on the local, regional and, ultimately, planetary level by a process of federation. Their ethos was from each according to their abilities, to each according to their need. The anarchists are a clear extension of the tradition of the people's utopia. Yet, despite their differences, and despite the denial of many Marxists, in a sense, so too is Marx himself.

If we view utopia as a cultural development that replaces the political association of the state as the organizing principle of society with a multiplicity of authentic social and economic associations, we gain a perspective that allows us to understand the utopian element in Marxism. While Marx never spelled out his "utopia" in concrete terms, he maintained that the new society must emerge from forms already present in the old. Certain writings are pregnant with implications of the form a post-revolutionary development might take. As Martin Buber points out, Marx's formulations concerning the "withering away of the state" point in a direction similar to that suggested by the anarchists. In his 1844 essay, "Critical Glosses," after discussing revolution as the last "political" act, Marx says, "But when its organizing activity begins, when its ultimate purpose, its soul emerges, socialism will throw the political husk away." Marx's belief in the ability of and need for the proletariat to seize direct control of the organs of production is reflected in his attitude toward the Paris Commune of 1871, a historical model that was also claimed by the anarchists. Marx praises the Commune as an expression of "the self-government of the producers." He believed that ultimately "the communal constitution would have rendered up to the body social all the powers which have hitherto been devoured by the parasitic excrescence of the State which battens on society and inhibits its free movement."

Beyond Capital

According to Marx, capitalism must organize the forces of production before socialism can emerge. Still, in a letter to Vera Zasulich, Marx contradicts his own statements when he discusses the prospects of adopting the cooperative tradition of the *mir*, the Russian peasant community, as a basis for socialism, and he indicates that such communal forms would prove valuable as models for the new society and in fact might be able to transcend the development of capitalism and move directly into communism. Here Marx was not advocating a return to primitive village communism, but rather the integration of the tradition of cooperation and communal ownership at a higher level of development into the new society.

Further indication of the utopian element in Marx's theories can be found in the section of the *Grundrisse* discussing pre-capitalist economic formations. Marx's descriptions of the institutions of primitive communism and their evolution into those of capitalism communicate a sense of the respect that he had for those earliest economic forms. In the dialectical formulations concerning the emergence of socialism from capitalism, it is possible once again to get a sense of the reemergence of the communist impulse, latent in society for epochs, on a higher level, set free by the development of material conditions that provide the preconditions for socialism. The impulse is not a mechanical application of tribal, communal organization but an unfolding of the same human potential in a new set of economic conditions.

Marx does not look to a change in human nature as the catalyst to bring socialism into being, but rather to the maturation of material conditions. In reference to the Paris Commune he says, "It has no ideals to realize, it has only to set free those elements of the new society which have already developed in the womb of the collapsing bourgeois society." Marx avoided any but the sketchiest intimations of what the "developed elements" might be, beyond the organization of the proletariat provided by the factory system, but he leaves no question as to the composition of the new society. It is "classless" in the sense that the class antagonisms between proletariat and bourgeois will be resolved by the elimination of the bourgeoisie, and it will be organized by the workers themselves. Marx's critical attitude toward the early utopians and all socialists who proposed complete "systems" for the new society is reflected in his unwillingness to draw his own blueprint. He focuses his attention instead on the process through which the new society can be actualized. It is, significantly, in the realm of process that his vision departs from the tradition of utopianism.

In the creation of the increasingly rigid and reified body of theoretical work that forms the basis of his political legacy, most noticeably in *Das Kapital*, Marx betrays his own utopian promise. In his search for a science with regular "predictable laws" and a universal, inexorable dialectic, he commits the very error for which Engels chastised the French utopians; he creates a rigid system that, despite many valuable insights, allows for no deviation and that fully incorporates Marx's own idiosyncrasies. Despite his unwillingness to blueprint his utopia, by the "scientific" pretense of his endeavor and by thus enshrining the limitations of his thought, Marx doomed his followers to a betrayal of his utopian impulse.

Marx's utopianism is in a certain sense the most interesting, provocative and inspiring aspect of his vast, often contradictory volume of work. This is the core of Marx's humanism and the engine that drives forward his revolutionary project. It is the positivistic "science" of Marx that has prevented the realization of this utopian core, and allowed for its distortion by the various parties and sects that bear his name.

As Ernst Bloch points out in his *Philosophy of the Future*, "A distinction has to be made between the Utopistic and the Utopian; the one approaches circumstances only immediately and abstractly, in order to improve them in a purely cerebral fashion, whereas the other has always brought along the constructural equipment of externality." He explains that "only Utopism, as it reaches out abstractly above reality, need not fight shy of a mere empiricism that undertakes only another form of abstract apprehension below reality. A real Utopian critique can only proceed from a viewpoint that is adequate, that does not—so to speak—correct or even replace over flying by a factistic creeping."

Certainly, this sense of Marx's critique of capitalism can be seen as utopian. The utopian perspective is able to provide a valuable critique because it exists outside of the given. Unlike ideology, utopia is a projection of that which does not yet exist, rather than a reflection of the ruling class and the dominant culture. As such, it is exempt from decay. In Bloch's paraphrase, "Only that which has never yet come to pass cannot grow old." Bloch concurs with the view that the urge to utopia is a primal one, discernible from the earliest epochs to the present, though represented by different forms in different historical situations. However, he sees continuity between the various aspects which utopia presents. The urge toward utopia, the vision of an ideal, harmonized society, ever shimmering on the horizon, is in Bloch' s view an archetype, which precedes even formalized mythology. Bloch identifies Marx as an heir to that tradition. It is the promise of utopia, not its specific image, which gives urgency to the Marxist project. That promise, while never crystallized, is central to understanding the dynamics of revolution.

In a letter to Arnold Ruge, the young Marx explains that, "Our slogan, therefore, must be: Reform of consciousness, not through dogmas, but through analysis of the mystical consciousness that is unclear about itself, whether in religion or politics. It will be evident then that the world has long dreamed of something of which it only has to become conscious in order to possess it in actuality." It will be evident, he continues, "that there is not a big blank between the past and the future, but rather that it is a matter of realizing the thoughts of the past. It will be evident finally that mankind does not begin any new work but performs its old work consciously," and thus "to have its sins forgiven, mankind has only to proclaim them for what they are."

In terms of his critique and his implicit vision, then, even Marx must be understood to contain an element that is utopian. This is not to say that the various hues of Marxists populating the left today have retained this utopian impulse. Orthodox Marxism, as practiced by "socialist" states and parties, however, is certainly distinct from the utopian praxis of people's movements.

"People's movements" are an expression of a different set of organizing principles. This is exemplified by the three interrelated questions that split the Marxists from the anarchists. The first question concerned the *constituency* of the movement—whether it was constituted by proletarians or whether it was based on a broader constitution of proletarians and déclassé intellectuals, peasants, petit bourgeoisie, as well as lumpen elements. The second question concerned the *structure* of the movement—whether it should be decentralized or centralized; and third questions concerned the role of the *state* and *politics*—dictatorship of the proletariat versus decentralized federation, party versus movement, and political economy versus holistic socio-economic-cultural reconstruction. Closely related to these major differences are questions about the forms of ownership and decision-making—as in nationalization versus collectivization, and central planning versus self-management. Although the relationship between the two positions has been historically complex and hard and fast categorizations are difficult, these remain the pivotal questions. From the time of the Paris Commune on, we can clearly note this bifurcation. Movements who insist on decentralization and reject the framework of the nation state, as well as parliamentary "political" activity as a valid means for cultural reconstruction, seem to be the more direct line of connection to the utopian continuum.

Utopian Moments

Given the historical trajectory of the libertarian wing of the utopian tradition, it is not surprising that there has been an association of the anarchist and reconstructive aspects with the radical ecology movement. Aspects of the tradition that bear a direct relation to the more conscious and radical elements in this ecology movement grow out of the theoretical congruence of concerns which transcend gross economic issues to examine the over all quality of life. The utopian—particularly the anarchist—concern for a process and organization that embodies the ideals of the new society is an obvious point of connection. The most profound insights of the utopians contain a core of logic that seems almost prescient when one considers that the concerns were addressed and articulated by a movement that existed hundreds of years before the word "ecology" entered our vocabulary.

In its concern with the whole of people's lives and its refusal to opt for the simplistic reductionism of the more mechanical "scientific view," the utopian tradition displayed an intuitive understanding of the holistic approach embodied in ecology as a scientific discipline. The perception of society as a whole and the concern of the utopian impulse with the transformation of the whole, rather than the reform of its parts, is reflected in the understanding that grows out of the study of ecology: that there are critical interdependencies and relationships in any system, social or ecological, that create a totality greater than the sum of its parts. The integration of components, the awesome display of unity growing from the diversity of nature, provides a powerful paradigm for the understanding of social interactions. This shared outlook, this concern with whole systems, is the underlying connection between the utopian tradition and the radical ecology movement, but it is further refined by a whole set of particulars that the two share as well. It must be understood, however, that the "laws" of natural ecology that influence the vision of the ecology movement are paradigmatic, powerful metaphors for the harmonious, homeostatic reworking envisioned by the radical ecology movement.

In that reworking, we could do well to reconsider the role of utopia, for as Bloch points out, "Utopian consciousness remains wholly without description inasmuch as the moment of its fulfillment is still outstanding." This "Utopian consciousness," he continues, "does not obscure its blinding goal with solutions, let alone with more reified means from the route to that goal." Its reason for doing so are not skeptical or agnostic, but "superlatively real." The "most objective correlative ground that Utopian consciousness possesses," Bloch claims, is that "the world substance, mundane matter itself, is not yet finished and complete, but exists in a Utopian—open state," that is to say in "a state in which its self-identity is not yet manifest."

SOCIAL ECOLOGY: AN ECOLOGICAL HUMANISM

Social ecology begins with an exploration of the past in order to gain an epistemological understanding into how humanity defines, and thus constitutes, nature. This is a question of vital importance, not merely an exercise in philosophical abstraction. The way we conceptualize nature and humanity's place in nature has become a highly contentious issue in ecological thought and environmental philosophy. The conclusions that we draw will inform our ethics and the political decisions that shape our world.

How can we derive such an epistemology? We must start out by understanding that nature is not a static entity but evolutionary, indeed, that the very process of biological evolution *constitutes* nature. The evolutionary record, natural history, is the reality of nature. From the molecular to the biospheric level, nature is in a process of constant flux and change: birth, death, mutation, even extinction are all part of a process which creates the complex web of life, of which humanity is a part. In biological terms, then, nature is both being and becoming. Evolution *is* nature.

First Nature and Humanity

Humanity must be placed within the evolutionary matrix and recognized as playing a unique role in that matrix by virtue of our capacity for both creative and destructive interaction with the rest of nature. As a species we have the ability to profoundly affect other species, ecosystems, and the biosphere itself in ways unparalleled by any other life form. This makes us both an integral part of nature—a product of the same evolutionary forces that created all other species on the planet, past and present—and at the same time distinct in our ability to affect nature. Social ecology recognizes this fact, compelling us to make a distinction between what we term "first nature," nature evolving according to processes not affected by humanity, and "second nature," which is nature determined by human consciousness and action.

In first nature a primary mode of evolution is natural selection: species change or mutate over time in order to adapt to the environment in which they find themselves, thus conferring an evolutionary advantage that ensures survival and regeneration. At some point cultural evolution emerges out of—though it does not replace—biological evolution. Second nature is best characterized by the emergence of self-consciousness and culture. Humanity remakes itself constantly through processes of tool making (technology), institution building, explanation (religion, philosophy, and science), and art. As humanity advances our understanding of the evolutionary process, of physics, genetics, and other arenas of science our species is becoming, at least potentially, to use Johann Gottlieb Fichte's phrase, "nature rendered self-conscious," nature aware of itself and consciously forming its own development. To an unprecedented degree, and with a rapidity seen nowhere else in nature, humanity adapts the environment to meet its needs: cultural evolution is a remarkably dynamic process capable of transforming the conditions of a society in less than a generation.

If we acknowledge the reality of a second nature, produced by human creativity and artifice, as distinct from first nature, we must also acknowledge that it grows directly out of first nature, or biological evolution. Thus, logically, first nature contained within itself, from its very inception, the potential for second nature. Natural history, the evolutionary record, must be read as a process in which nothing essential is lost. Second nature still contains within it first nature; complex forms of mammalian life begin as single cells and organize into more complex cellular forms (organs) contained within still more complex assemblages of cells (organisms). The pH of the ancient oceans in which life first began is replicated in the amniotic fluid that supports life in the womb of complex mammals, like human beings. In a certain sense the conception, gestation, and birth of an individual person roughly replicates the process of biological evolution. Our species comprises both first nature and second nature.

When we view the evolutionary record over the whole of biological development we see a movement toward an ever-greater degree of diversity and complexity of life forms, and the potentiality for consciousness and self-consciousness. This is not to say that there is a linear, unbroken ascent toward human consciousness; evolution is full of fits and starts, florescence and decline, even extinction. But it is undeniable that life on earth evolved from unconscious, single-celled organisms, to biologically complex forms of life with the capacity to think abstractly and to reason. Does this fact confer upon humanity the "crown of creation," the right to dominate the rest of nature and view first nature as mere resource? Or does it require us to understand ourselves as a part of nature with the capacity to play either a destructive role or a creative and sustaining role? Does this understanding not bring with it the responsibility to critically examine the existing relationship between first and second nature, particularly in light of the insights offered by the science of ecology? And should we not create an ethics and politics that can ensure a reharmonization of first and second nature to stem the tide of destruction resulting from our current ethics and politics, which threaten the integrity of both first nature and second nature?

Social ecology suggests that we need to look at first nature to gain insight into the principles that inform natural history and ensure ecosystem health. Such an examination must draw on the best scientific understanding and interpretation we can assemble, but we must also recognize that such a project is not purely empirical. The history of interpretation of "the laws of nature" is fraught with highly subjective, politically charged moments. In the nineteenth century, Social Darwinists like Herbert Spencer twisted Darwin's ideas to provide a rationale for British colonialism and imperialism. More recently, Hitler justified his views by drawing on the "immutable laws of nature." In light of this history, rather than claim immutability or absolute authority, social ecology attempts to use the best existing science to identify tendencies or principles at work in evolutionary processes and ecosystem dynamics, and acknowledges that these tendencies may be mutable and do not exhaust the whole range of processes at work in first nature. They do seem, however, to represent important tendencies that relate directly to the project of reharmonizing first and second nature, a project that takes on some urgency given the current threats facing the planet. We must also recognize, as with any theory based on science, that social ecology too will require modification as new scientific insights emerge.

Ecological Ethics and Society

An ethics that has a goal to reharmonize first and second nature must be oriented toward encouraging ever-greater complexity, diversity, and higher degrees of consciousness. This orientation must inform its relation to both first and second nature, striving to protect and create ecosystems that offer a multiplicity of trophic levels to support biologically diverse species in a set of complex interactions, and do so in a highly self-conscious fashion.

The same principles must be applied in the realm of second nature. If our goal is an ecological society our ethics must ensure complex, diverse societies and cultures that encourage ever-greater degrees of human self-consciousness, characterized by respect, participation, equity, and scientific understanding. The pursuit of ever-greater degrees of complexity, diversity and freedom (as consciousness and choice) is a necessary condition for both healthy ecosystems and healthy societies, and a precondition for the reharmonization of first and second nature.

A related principle present in first nature that must necessarily be applied to human societies in order to achieve a healthy relationship between the two is the principle of unity in diversity. The health, strength, and stability of an ecosystem stand in direct relation to the diversity of species that interact within the system. Ecosystems with the highest degree of biodiversity, like rainforests or estuaries, are able to sustain themselves for thousands of years. Large numbers of species fill every trophic level, giving the system as a whole the ability to compensate for even vast fluctuations in the population of any particular species, therefore allowing it to maintain its overall stability and integrity.

An application of this principle is an ethical imperative in second nature, where lack of unity and intolerance of diversity pose a threat not only to individual cultures and societies but to the biosphere as a whole. The results of second nature's unwillingness to embrace this principle has led to social and ecological disaster alike; warfare, genocide, and racism in second nature, and a frightening diminution of biodiversity, a wholesale destruction of ecosystems, and global climate change, in first nature. The two are inextricably linked, and social ecology demands a recognition and implementation of the principle of unity in diversity as a corrective to the destruction that has already been wrought.

Hierarchy and Evolution

When the science of ecology began its study of ecosystems the tendency was to view systemic relations in hierarchical terms; a central concept in understanding ecosystem dynamics was that of the food chain, a rigid hierarchy of dependencies in which the largest carnivores were placed at the top. As our scientific understanding has increased, this crude model has been replaced by more sophisticated descriptions that define the complex interrelationships at work in an ecosystem as a food web. The food web describes an essentially non-hierarchical network of relationships based on interdependencies, linking together all species into a mutually supportive whole. This has led to a recognition that first nature is organized non-hierarchically.

The hierarchies that we establish between species in first nature—the lion as "king of beasts," or the "lowly ant"— are really a projection of human hierarchies. In a technical sense, hierarchy is defined as an institutionalized system of command and control that ultimately has recourse to physical coercion in order to compel obedience. No such systems exist in first nature. The lion does not command and control any other species, nor do lions institutionalize their relationships. Even the seemingly dominant role that an individual female lion may play within her pride is better understood as a form of situational dominance than an institutionalized hierarchy.

Hierarchy vitiates the mutualistic web of relationships crucial to ecosystem stability and even survival. The recurrent cycles of birth, death, and decay link all of first nature and second nature. Despite the undeniable role played by inter- and intra-species competition for evolutionary advantage, ecosystem dynamics are best characterized as rooted in the principle of mutualism; each species plays a critical role in the health and development of the other. This is true even in predator-prey relationships where various species are mutually dependent: put somewhat simplistically, predator species depend on prey for survival, and the prey is dependent on the predator for maintaining healthy population levels. The mutualistic relationships at work in an ecosystem become more complex in direct proportion to the biodiversity of the system.

Evolution is, above all, the realm of potentiality. Every life form contains within it a set of possibilities, both biological and behavioral. These potentialities and the striving to actualize them are what drive life forward. The degree to which this process is conscious is a major factor in natural history and one way that we can begin to differentiate second nature from first nature. This is not to suggest a radical disjuncture between first and second nature: although first nature is always present in second nature we can see a gradual emergence of consciousness, self-consciousness, and human efforts to fulfill inherent potentialities that characterizes the emergence of culture. If mutualism is to serve as a natural tendency that informs human ethics, it must be rooted in this understanding of potentiality; it must be a part of the continuum of behaviors that make us human. This potentiality has found wide expression throughout the whole of human history, which itself offers convincing evidence that we must incorporate this principle into an ethical framework that will allow us to fully reharmonize first and second nature.

The popular conception of an immutable human nature based on greed, competition, warfare, and domination is challenged by the anthropological record. Indeed, anthropology forces us to reject such a narrow view of "human nature," and to replace it with the much broader concept of a continuum of potential human behaviors. This concept, while undeniably including the potentiality for greed, competition, warfare, and domination, also includes the potentiality for caring, sharing, mutualism, and non-hierarchical relationships. This framework provides a real basis for believing that our species, humanity, has the potentiality to create an ecological society. Anthropologists have identified these ecological behaviors as central in many forms of human society, primarily those rooted in pre-capitalist systems of production. These traits represent a potentiality for the future. I do not mean to suggest that our species could, or would want to, return to hunting and gathering: there can be no return. Rather, I would say that these forms of behavior represent principles. With human creativity and invention we can apply these principles in ways appropriate to modern life.

Cultures and societies have always reinforced and rewarded particular forms of behavior and devalued others. Through the processes of socialization and formal education our society has chosen to reinforce and reward ecologically destructive relationships and patterns of behavior, and furthermore to reify them into "human nature." An awareness of the other potentialities embodied in our humanity gives hope that a transformation of those patterns may occur. Although by no means guarantied or preordained, social ecology argues that such a transformation *must* occur if we are to truly achieve our potential to become "nature rendered self-conscious," thus reharmonizing first and second nature and resolving the ecological crises that threaten our existence.

From Ecology to Politics

A transformation of this magnitude requires a radically new vision and program: a new ecological epistemology, an ethics rooted in principles derived from first nature, and a bold social-political praxis. We must be willing to undertake a searching examination of the *roots* of the ecological crisis, using the ethical principles that we derive from our understanding of nature. Such an examination leads us from the realm of traditional environmentalism, still rooted in a dualistic epistemology that views "nature" as a collection of natural resources, to a social ecology that promises a fundamental reharmonization of first and second nature.

Indeed, this recognition calls for political solutions that go far beyond the "band aid" approach advocated by most environmentalists. It requires that we resolve the social crises that are the underlying causes of our various environmental crises. It suggests that healthy ecosystems and a healthy relationship between first and second nature only can result from an ecological society, and that such an ecological society must be an ethical community, rooted in the ethical principles that we derive from our understanding of first nature itself.

The ecological crisis demands more that a change in consciousness. Though such a change is necessary, it is not, in and of itself, sufficient. We must also begin to undertake action informed by a consciousness rooted in a social ecology. To be sure, the process of ecological reconstruction will not be an easy one: it will require major shifts in thinking and in social organization, as well as the use of new, ecologically sound technologies and techniques. We must begin the process of ecological reconstruction by preserving existing ecosystems to ensure their integrity and to draw upon them as reservoirs of biodiversity. We must ensure that no more species are lost. It is also crucial to engage in ecological restoration to the extent that we are able, restoring damaged ecosystems to their previous state. This in turn suggests that we need to explore and implement new, ecological models for development, a community-based process that both meets human needs and respects and restores ecosystems. This critical reconstructive dimension must be fully articulated and applied within the ethical framework presented by evolution.

This reconstructive project is a crucial element in the development of a social ecology: it is not enough to philosophize, we must act. Our actions, however, must be informed by ethics and scientific understanding. Mindless or insufficiently considered action may indeed make our situation worse, instead of improving it. The ends that we seek—societies moving toward ever-greater complexity, diversity, and freedom, creating unity through diversity and mutualistic organization, and highly self-conscious about their relationship to first nature—can only be brought about by social movements that reflect and embody those same principles. Ends and means must be congruent.

Action rooted in social ecology demands broad participation and democracy. All around the world, local communities are already challenging the irrational culture of destruction. The struggles of indigenous farmers in Mexico fighting to save their rainforests, peasants in Nepal fighting to prevent the damming of rivers, and poor black communities in Louisiana fighting to close down toxic chemical plants are all part of the same global movement. So too are urban homesteaders in devastated Detroit neighborhoods reclaiming abandoned buildings, and youth groups growing organic vegetables on vacant lots in New York City. They stand together with the millions around the world who protest a rapacious world economy dominated by giant corporations.

These combinations of protest and reconstructive action are only fledgling steps in what must become a larger and broader movement, but they are promising nonetheless. They point the way toward new organizational models that embody the ecological ethics necessary to achieve a reharmonization of first and second nature. They are diverse, decentralized, non-hierarchical, and participatory, and represent a new model for social action that can begin to counter the destructive path of the dominant culture.

Toward a New Enlightenment

A perspective informed by social ecology must also address the future, and it must do so in a manner that draws on the ethical principles derived from first nature. It is insufficient to extrapolate the present into the future, as futurists and systems theorists do. Any discussion of the future, if it is to be ecological, must be rooted in the concept of potentiality, an understanding of what could be. Evolution itself is a process of unfolding potentiality on a biological level: of organisms either fulfilling their potential for growth, development, and reproduction, or failing to do so. Potentiality should not be equated with inevitability; many factors influence whether it is actualized or not. Social ecology examines the future by trying to tease out potentialities for ecological restoration and a reharmonization of first and second nature, while working to actualize those potentialities.

By doing so, social ecology draws on one of the great traditions of humanity, utopian thinking, which is based on an understanding of the potentialities inherent, though unrealized, in the present. During the Renaissance and the Enlightenment, utopian thinking emerged as one of the most important forms of both social criticism and speculation about possible new forms of social organization. It was used to explore the far shores of human possibilities; to inspire people to transcend the limitations of their severely limited societies. But utopian thinking offers more than inspiration: it also offers a sense of orientation. Without a vision of the type of society we desire, it will be impossible to ever achieve it. In a modern ecological context, the details of those utopian principles, rooted in a scientific understanding of ecosystems, will be applied through democratically developed plans at the local level.

Social ecology examines the future from this perspective and recognizes the real, existing potentiality for an ecological society. Utilizing modern scientific insights and technics we have the potential to solve the world's ecological problems; we can create and utilize non-polluting, renewable sources of energy; we can reverse the process of global climate change; we can restore damaged ecosystems and ensure continued biodiversity; we can end pollution and clean up toxic wastes; and we can provide a healthy diet for the world's population. Today, all of this is possible by utilizing existing technologies.

For the first time in the history of the planet we now have the capacity to eliminate scarcity. Our society has the technology and science required to meet the needs of all humanity for food, shelter, and energy. What we lack is the social vision and the political will to do so. Hierarchical concentrations of wealth and power have led to a catastrophic imbalance in the distribution of resources around the planet. The gap between rich and poor has been steadily increasing in recent decades. Just as the Enlightenment led to a restructuring of society that shook the foundations of the old social order, a new Enlightenment rooted in a social ecology must aim for the same. I am painfully aware of the limitations and many problematic aspects of the original Enlightenment, and I am not arguing that we should replicate the content, but rather that it represents a process from which we must learn.

The Enlightenment project began with a set of ideas that offered a radical critique of what was, and a transcendent vision of what could be and what should be, rooted in a new ethical framework. A similar process is urgently needed today if the potentiality for an ecological society is to ever be realized. To fail to do so is to abandon our humanity and enter headlong into an era of unprecedented ecological devastation.

EDUCATION FOR SOCIAL CHANGE

The social and ecological crises we face require new thinking and creative solutions. Those solutions will only grow out of an educational process, and it has to be education of a particular type. It is imperative that we now re-examine our basic notions of what constitutes an education. What are we educating people for? How can we equip people with the critical thinking skills required to change the trajectory of our culture?

I would suggest that traditional education is not really education at all. What passes for education in our public schools and in most of our private schools—and certainly in our universities and colleges today—is in fact a sort of training. It has very little to do with allowing for the unfolding of potentialities within the individual, which I see as the basis for real education, and the formation of ecologically responsible community members. It is, rather, an attempt to reinforce the hegemonic culture and to reproduce its structures of hierarchy and domination. Today more than ever, students are being tested, sorted, and inculcated with the ideology of capitalism. The aim is to train willing young minds to meet the needs of corporations and industry by producing students who unquestioningly go out, join the work force and become "productive" members of society. In the United States, there have been recent calls for curtailing support of the traditional liberal arts curriculum, and investing our resources exclusively in training in math and science, in order for our country to "remain competitive."

Given the direction in which society is moving today—toward ecological catastrophe—the last thing we need to do is reproduce the system. We need instead to generate approaches to education that help transform that system and change its basic structures. Traditional education operates on a variety of levels, and we have to understand how those levels reinforce each other. This problem must be confronted in a critical fashion, one that recognizes that beyond teaching particular skills and techniques, contemporary education reinforces the hegemony of capital and socializes students in the habits of obedience and acquiescence. These behaviors are modeled day after day in classrooms and lecture halls, and students who fail to get the message are disciplined and humiliated.

Traditional Education

More than anything, the very *form* of traditional education is intended to drill students into a culture of unquestioning obedience and passivity. They are taught to sit in orderly rows in classrooms, they are taught to respond to bells and whistles, and to never question the authority of the teacher. In the early grades the teacher's primary role in education is maintaining order in the classroom. It has very little to do with learning at all. Actually, that attempt to reproduce the order of our hierarchical society; to create obedience to authority and compliant students who become willing workers, is extremely destructive. It squelches initiative, discourages questioning, rewards conformity, and all too frequently determines, at an early age, whether a child will "succeed" or not. This behavioral modification and a child's reaction to it then becomes a self-fulfilling prophecy: in the higher grades and in college and university, the perception of the student's capacity, and, all too often, the students own self-image is shaped by these early classroom experiences. Questioning and resisting authority are seen as signs of deep emotional problems. Indeed, the emphasis on obedience has given rise to a newly discovered psychological condition: ODD, Oppositional Defiant Disorder. A basic developmental process of childhood—questioning authority—is now being defined as a disease!

The regimentation of the earlier grades is carried on with a vengeance as students progress through their educational career. They come to accept the perspective of their teachers, and grades are used as a cudgel to maintain their teachers' authority. At the university level, the enormity of the lecture halls and the anonymity of the student reinforce the received wisdom of the dominant culture. Here, the emphasis on training for careers becomes a mania, and the pressure of paying back huge student loans tends to further narrow a student's focus and sense of possibilities. And we now see how corporate interests hold colleges and universities in thrall, and, through funding and joint ventures, increasingly shape their research agendas and curricula.

So what are students actually being taught? Undeniably, it's useful for young people to learn how to read and how to write, and how to do basic mathematical calculations. These are all things that will serve them well, and should be part of any curriculum. But beyond that, there is also a *hidden* curriculum: the basic assumptions of the dominant culture are grafted into the very character structure of the students, with devastating effects for both the individuals being "taught" and for our society as a whole.

And more than ever, we are seeing the corporate agenda enter directly into the classroom, as pre-programmed, packaged curricula that make it very easy for a teacher—by using these "enrichment" opportunities for students—to bring home the message of capitalism and the corporate world. I saw this very strikingly when I took my elementary-aged daughters to the American Museum of Natural History in New York some years ago. We went into the Hall of Biodiversity, a multimillion-dollar exhibit sponsored by the Monsanto Corporation, Citibank and the Rockefeller Fund. It was a huge hall, with millions of dollars worth of exhibits, intended primarily to educate young children about the need for biodiversity, and about the ecological crisis that the planet is facing. But in that whole entire hall there was not a single mention of corporations and not one word about capitalism. The fact that today's crisis can be traced directly back to corporations and capitalism does not enter into the discourse to which our children are exposed. And there were busloads of kids going through the hall, with well-meaning teachers, no doubt. But this basic outlook is never challenged—it's not even questioned—and thus the hegemonic nature of capitalism is reinforced.

This brings us to another level on which we have to understand traditional education, and that is the *intentionality* with which children are educated today. This intentionality is not concerned with the individual students, their needs, their wellbeing, and the unfolding of their particular potentialities. It is, rather, a cookie cutter model of education, which follows the agenda of the corporations and the capitalist system. It reflects and reinforces the class divisions that riddle our society. In the United States this is very obvious: by and large the children of the poor are educated for work in the trades or the service sector, and those of the wealthy sent to elite universities and prepared for management or professional positions.

So what is the alternative? If we accept the idea that meaningful social change will only come about through a process of education, which is, of course, one of the underlying beliefs of social ecology, then we need to look very carefully at what constitutes a radical education. What kind of education would be able to bring about the social change necessary to reverse the engines of destruction that are literally eroding three and a half billion years of biological evolution on this

163

planet? How can we create a *radical* education? I suggest the very same categories we use to understand traditional education must be applied to explain radical education.

Radical Education

For an education to be truly radical we first need to examine the form it takes. How can the structures of learning be altered to encourage creativity, questioning, and critical thinking? To be sure, there is not a single solution or a single model that would constitute a radical education. Individual students have individual learning styles and our education should reflect this. No single approach meets the needs of all students, and students at different developmental stages respond to different approaches to teaching and learning. Radical education requires a student-centered approach, and this is something traditional classrooms cannot provide. Such an approach undermines the authoritarian mechanisms that govern contemporary classrooms and replaces the modern "teach to the test" education, and its hidden curriculum of obedience and discipline.

A student-centered education means that students are encouraged to pursue their interests, and teachers provide resources to aid them in their pursuit: they should help students identify important questions, help them to acquire the skills they need, and offer guidance and critique along the way. As we know from studies of development in early childhood and adolescence, there are various stages at which particular kinds of teaching and learning are appropriate. At the level of elementary education, I would suggest that the primary need of children is a type of free and unfettered development and education that is very rare today. Certainly there are oases around the world; there is a free school here or a free school there. But in general these noble experiments are isolated and the number of children that they reach is extremely limited. And that is unfortunate, because at this formative stage in children's development the most valuable thing we can offer them is freedom to explore, and resources they can use in that exploration. This is not something that figures largely in traditional education schemes at all.

Learning is not limited to the classroom; in fact a radical education must recognize that the local community and the natural world offer tremendous opportunities for learning. Participatory and experiential learning are powerful adjuncts to more conventional forms of education. The stimulation offered by taking teaching and learning into the community and bringing the community into the classroom helps students engage with the larger world.

As children develop we can begin to also look at how their interests as students evolve. Typically today, the subject matter being studied helps to reinforce the hidden curriculum. In the United States, as students go through traditional high schools they are taught with text books that talk about Christopher Columbus as discovering the New World, and say very little about the oppression and the slaughter of Native Americans that accompanied the "age of discovery." Instead of learning about the deleterious effects of colonialism and imperialism, we celebrate the great warriors and conquistadores who brought the benefits of European civilization to the rest of the world. We valorize the founding fathers, but never mention that many of them were slave owners, and we never question why there were no founding mothers.

Any kind of radical education has to expose students to a hidden history: the stories of those who paid the price of conquest, whose voices are silenced by conventional history. We have to ensure that students are exposed to a history that reflects a critical view of modernity and the development that we so blithely assume to be inevitable. Students need to know the history of resistance, to understand cultures that are organized around very different sets of principles than our own, and to be exposed to the lives of people who questioned the status quo; this is not part of the standard curricula in any high school that I know of today.

This question of *content* is closely wedded to the form of the education; they mutually reinforce the foundational hierarchy of our society. Today, students are exposed to curricula that offer the analyses and perspectives of the dominant culture. For example, in the Hall of Biodiversity at the Museum of Natural History there was an emphasis on overconsumption as a pressing ecological problem. Blame was placed exclusively on the individual—the analysis presented suggested that we are all greedy consumers and that is why we have an environmental crisis. The crisis exists because each one of us consumes too much, and the problem will become worse because the world is becoming overpopulated. The "greedy consumers" are to blame, whether they are driving SUVs in America or trying to find enough food to survive in Africa, no differentiation was made. Such an analysis is grossly inadequate and does nothing to prepare young people, or anyone for that matter, to make sense out of the mess that we are in today. Rather, it mystifies it and ensures the continuation of a system in which the elites benefit at the expense of the poor. And that's very much the intentionality of traditional education. So, if we are to help students to develop their critical faculties, and the ability to draw their own conclusions so they can contribute to a larger project of social change, they must be given an adequate historical grounding and the tools needed to critique the contemporary system.

Indeed, from an ecological perspective, a radical education should encourage students to look critically not just at the impact of their individual decisions as consumers, not just at how they pollute, but rather how the dominant culture produces the conditions that make pollution inevitable. It is important that students understand the underlying sources of the problem, and not the fact that they aren't recycling enough paper. Because, in truth, the pollution created by a reader of this book over their lifetime is insignificant compared to the pollution created by one day of production at the International Paper Plant in Glens Falls, New York. We need to develop educational processes and curricula that give students exposure to the ideas, concepts, and critical understanding that will allow them to begin to deconstruct the mythology supporting the current system. This is crucial if we are ever to change that system and replace it with something positive and life-affirming.

Education at the ISE

The Institute for Social Ecology is committed to radical education and utilizes many different approaches to learning. Since 1974 we have offered a wide range of programs and a variety of formats, from workshops and single lectures to conferences and longer intensive seminars. In addition to programs based on our own campus in Vermont, we have offered programs at numerous colleges and universities, as well as in communities all around the country, from New York City to Seattle. Our work focuses on the concrete skills needed to participate actively in movements for the creation of an ecological society.

Our classes are small and often discussion-based. Students in our campus-based programs also take part in weekly community meetings, which establish the norms for campus life and policies related to the particular program. Students, faculty, and staff set the agenda for the community meetings and bring forward their concerns, and together, through face-to-face discussions, we find common solutions. The ISE itself is an institution that operates democratically, both in setting policy and defining programs. Students are encouraged to participate in that process, gaining experience in the practice of direct democracy. This institutional commitment to prefigurative politics is conceived as an essential part of a student's education. Involvement in the governance of the ISE gives students a real voice in determining all aspects of their education, and helps to create an environment of mutual respect in which they are truly empowered to help define the content of their learning.

Although we emphasize alternative education, I think it is very important that we have provided credit-bearing and degree-granting programs for both graduate and undergraduate students. These courses of study present an alternative to more traditional institutions of higher learning, and have provided a forum for educating people who will become educators and organizers themselves. In these programs students individually design a course of study that can include discussion-based classes, lectures, experiential learning, community involvement, independent study, and research. Often their studies include critical reflection on activist projects in which they are involved. We have also insured that our programs are available to people regardless of their financial ability, and have tried, with varying degrees of success, to recruit a truly diverse student body.

In addition to the radical institutional setting offered by the ISE and its non-hierarchical formats for teaching and learning, our programs also present radical content. We seek to lay the groundwork for students to develop analyses from a perspective that is both critical and utopian, one that challenges the shibboleths of capitalism and transcends the limitations of the given. We strive to help students "make sense" out of a world that seems increasingly beyond our comprehension. Our courses thus cover a broad array of topics, ranging from nature philosophy and ecological ethics, to practical politics and community activism. We explore hierarchy and domination in many of its manifestations—such as colonialism, racism, sexism, heterosexism, antisemitism, and class oppression—utilizing philosophy, anthropology, history, and sociology to deepen our understanding of those phenomena and to analyze ways to combat them. We try to unearth the "hidden history" of our own communities, and any active or vestigial manifestations of mutual aid and cooperation that might help in their reconstruction. We look at politics from both a critical and a reconstructive perspective:

we explore the concept and history of direct democracy, and try to extract lessons from radical movements that can inform our own practice.

The ISE has also offered a series of classes in "applied social ecology," often incorporating experiential, hands-on approaches to learning. In the 1970s we offered pioneering classes in solar energy and wind power in which students built fully functional energy systems from the bottom up. Students have also designed and built energy efficient buildings on our campus as part of their course work, and they have developed organic gardens for campus use as well as in their own communities. We integrate work in the community with work in the classroom and stress the interaction between theory and practice. All these classes provide practical skills that will be needed to create an ecological society.

Furthermore, we eschew testing and arbitrary measures of achievement, instead asking students to undergo a rigorous process of self-evaluation, and our faculty members also contribute to this evaluation. Rather than ranking and grading students these evaluations are our assessment mechanisms—individualized and qualitative—intended to help students recognize their strengths and weaknesses, and, most importantly, to help them further develop their insights and skills.

The form of education we offer at the ISE—open and flexible, student-centered and community-based, non-authoritarian and developmental—is meant to reinforce the lessons of the curriculum. The institutional setting itself is seen as prefiguring a cooperative, ecological society and offering another level of education for the participants. A diversity of strategies and tactics has grown out of our work, and a further refinement of the theories of social ecology is ongoing in light of those experiences.

Transforming the World

There is a great deal of intent behind traditional approaches to education; they know exactly what they are doing. We have to be equally intentional. I am not suggesting that we have to be dogmatic or sectarian, and that we have to limit expression or inquiry. Rather, we have to ensure that students are allowed to explore "subversive" and radical ideas, that they are exposed to alternative views of the world, that they are given access to the resources they need to sort things out, and that they come away with an understanding that helps them make sense out of a system that thrives on its own mystification. By providing our students with the ability to think critically and independently, to question authority, and to view themselves not as passive consumers but as active citizens, we can help them become agents of social change. They can all make a real difference in moving us toward an ecological society.

If we fail to do this, however, if we do not educate for social change, we will be condemning the world to simply reproducing, at ever-deepening levels of degradation, the system that exists today. Therefore, at the risk of sounding grandiose, I would argue that the real work of education should be nothing less than the transformation of the world. It is not a simple task, but it is vitally important, and it requires a concerted effort and a willingness to challenge

171

the assumptions of our current system at every level. To this end, I believe that each of us, as an individual, has a responsibility to serve as both a student and an educator.

Murray Bookchin once wrote, "Every revolutionary project is an educational project." But not every educational project is a revolutionary project. Education for social change requires a conscious effort to embody the principles of an ecological society in the form, content, and institutional structures of the education that we offer. We need to re-envision teaching and learning in a fashion that can help us to re-envision a new, ecological society.

OCCUPY YOUR
NEIGHBORHOOD

In the wake of the recent financial crises, a new social movement emerged—the Occupy movement—which was remarkably successful in attracting media and in the eyes of the public. The Occupy movement highlighted capitalism's inherent injustices, and its message resonated with a broad cross-section of the public. But the movement failed to establish a solid foothold. The initial media frenzy has subsided and Occupy activists are now struggling to develop new strategies to engage the 99% and to re-energize the movement.

My experience with Occupy (I was in Zucotti Park on the first day of the occupation and made several other visits to the encampment, participated in protest marches, General Assemblies and Working Committee meetings, and taught classes at three week-long seminars for Occupy organizers), and the meteoric rise and decline of the movement in the popular culture led me to reflect on the strengths and weaknesses of Occupy. Conceived as primarily a protest movement, Occupy is a testament to both the vision and spirit of its organizers, and the limitations of protest. The repression of the various physical occupations of public space in the United States and elsewhere undercut the primary vehicle of the occupiers and their presence on the ground in the face of the 1%, their allies, and hirelings.

Movement Democracy and Community Politics

The Occupy movement, with its emphasis on prefigurative politics, presented a model for how direct democracy can be applied in a movement setting and served as an inspiration both for participants and observers. However, as events unfolded the limitations of this approach were revealed. The open-ended nature of its general assemblies led to time-consuming and, for many, frustrating meetings dealing with formidable logistics of managing the encampments. Increasingly, tactical and strategic discussions were the province of working committees and other small groups. The fetishization of process played a role in the decline of Occupy's public presence, and led some people to question the efficacy of direct democracy. As important as directly democratic processes are in the movement context they do not constitute direct democracy, they constitute movement democracy. Movement democracy functions under duress, and makes decisions of a primarily tactical nature. Direct democracy functions in an entirely different fashion when it is based in a geographic community where people share their daily lives in an on going fashion, and think long term about the direction of their community.

This conflation of movement democracy with direct democracy can be confusing, and severely limits the movement's effectiveness, but at the same time, it also suggests an approach that might deepen and broaden Occupy's presence and impact. I believe we should understand the protest-oriented approach as part of a larger strategy for social change that links together oppositional and alternative movements, and takes them into the realm of politics.

Inspiring and exciting as moments like the occupation of Zuccotti Park and other public spaces are, they constitutes festivals of the oppressed, or in the lexicon of postmodern anarchism, "temporary autonomous zones." These are important spaces for learning and celebrating the spirit of revolt—they give us a glimpse of what could be—but they are by their very nature and definition illusory and momentary. The question that occupiers should be asking is not how we can create more of these moments, but rather, how the approaches we celebrate can become institutionalized: we should be asking how we can create *permanent* autonomous zones and expand them to encompass cities, regions, nations, and, ultimately, the globe. Are these goals grandiose and unrealistic? I do not think so. My personal experience with town meeting democracy in Vermont, and "town meetings" in New York's Loisaida neighborhood has convinced me that it is possible to create and empower local forums for directly democratic decision making in virtually any setting, and to use them as a means of both educating people in the practice of democracy, and helping them to affect their own lives in meaningful ways. This is the way we can begin to create the new sensibility required for the revolutionary restructuring of contemporary society.

It is time to extend the experience of the Occupy movement into new arenas and transcend the limitations of protest by applying direct democracy not just in our movements, not just in our encampments and at our protests, but where we live. It is time to occupy our neighborhoods, towns and villages; to take the lessons learned in the streets and in the parks to our own geographical communities. An old maxim suggests that all politics are local. Let us recognize that change of the magnitude required to mount an effective challenge to the capitalist system will require a majoritarian movement, and that it is a project which will demand the development of not only new institutions, but a new sense of community as well. This is certainly a daunting task, but such revolutionary changes in the underlying structures of society have occurred before, and they can occur again. It will take a concerted effort over an extended period of time, but it provides a clear path out of the conundrum in which we currently find ourselves mired.

The limitations of a purely oppositional movement, which is essentially what Occupy has been, have become clear. We need to combine protest with the creation of counter-institutions that empower people to make decisions that affect their communities and the larger society as well. Such a libertarian municipalist approach addresses the issue of power directly, something that a purely protest-based movement is unable to do. Libertarian municipalism attempts to engage with politics by redefining the dynamic of power. Rather than demanding redress and reform, this approach offers a revolutionary redefinition and transformation of politics.

Organizing of this type requires developing real relationships with ones neighbors. Participatory action research of the type practiced by Students for a Democratic Society in the mid sixties offers a good model for this work. Their Economic Research and Action Project brought collectives of young SDS organizers into a number of low-income communities where they worked with community members to identify issues they could address together. In addition to building relationships of solidarity in front-line communities, they were able to address the real needs of community members. Alliances created through such struggles could provide the basis for an effective and inclusive "town meeting" approach.

The need for a place-based politics rooted in direct democracy is the critical component largely missing in recent discussions of movement strategy. I emphasize this because I believe that community is the locus for real change from a centralized state to a decentralized, directly democratic society. I am referring here to a geographic community, be it an urban neighborhood, village or town. Genuine community-based organizing and activism is the only way to create direct, community-based democracy. This is where we can achieve

177

the human scale needed for face-to-face decision making and unmediated relationships of all types. Directly democratic forums like these have a deep and rich history. In the Western tradition we can look back to ancient Greece, the medieval folkmoot, and the New England town meeting, to name but a few examples. In fact, for almost the whole of human history, from the Paleolithic until the advent of civilization, many cultures are understood by anthropologists to be egalitarian, with all participating fully in the self-management of their society. Even today, most communities can identify at least vestigial institutions that embody that sensibility.

I do not assume that coherent communities exist everywhere, or that there are not communities rooted in exclusion rather than inclusion. In many cases we need to re-create connections between people, in other cases we need to combat racist, sexist, and reactionary attitudes of all types. Our role must be to organize and educate. In many communities, however, affective ties between people do exist, and there are many places where there are still vestiges of community life.

Community Organizing in Rural Vermont

Most communities offer at least rudimentary institutions and cultural traditions for direct civic participation. Let me now briefly explain how I apply these insights in practice. In addition to teaching and writing about social change, and participating in campaigns and protests, I live in Marshfield, Vermont, which is the second poorest town in Washington County. Most people live in mobile homes, run-down turn-of-the-century farmhouses and Section 8 rental housing.

People here work hard to scrape by at an annual household income that averages well under $50,000 a year. Marshfield is not an urban neighborhood, but a town with 1,300 residents.

Here in Marshfield I participate in our Town Meeting, which is a directly democratic form of town governance. At Town Meeting we make decisions about every facet of our community and consider resolutions on national policies like nuclear disarmament, genetic engineering, nuclear power, global warming, campaign finance reform, and any other issue citizens of the town care to raise. I also serve on the town energy committee, which has brought bus services to town, (admittedly more limited than we would like, but a step in the right direction); it has conducted energy surveys and efficiency updates, mostly for trailers and drafty old farmhouses owned by low income people; and it has offered forums on global warming, retrofitted town buildings for energy conservation, and created a tax district to help finance alternative energy in town. Currently it is installing solar photovoltaics to power public buildings, and is beginning to organize an energy co-op in town. Nothing revolutionary here, just working with people in directly democratic forums in a cooperative and mutualistic fashion around decisions that affect their lives. I believe this is all part of the long process of educating people about particular issues and learning together the actual process of practicing democracy. It is a way to build relationships of trust and mutual respect—a precondition for the kind of movement necessary to truly transform the system.

There are divisions in Marshfield, of course, but primarily of a class and ideological nature. I try to overcome these

179

divisions by actively working with people across those lines through forums like the town meeting, energy committee, and school board (to which I was elected and served on for three years), trying to find common ground, explore differences and convince others of my point of view. All of this is possible only because we live together in a community. I certainly recognize the difficulties people face in their neighborhoods and do not mean to minimize them. But there is a very strong sense of community here in Marshfield, continually expressed not only through town governance, but also through how we share tools, co-operates to maintain neighborhood trail systems, and gather regularly to celebrate our community.

I believe it is important to build on this sense of community and develop local traditions for sharing and improving people's quality of life. My experience in New York's Lower East Side in the 1970s was that it is possible to create alternatives that markedly improve people's lives and fight for social justice at the same time. In Loisaida people were able to cross racial, ethnic and class lines to create low-income co-ops in abandoned buildings, build community gardens in vacant lots, and create a myriad of cooperative enterprises, while holding town meetings and contesting for power with official city planning agencies. There the struggle against gentrification was waged when these positive actions made the neighborhood attractive to gentrifiers. By the 1980s the forces of gentrification had won and the poor were largely replaced by Yuppies. The only projects that remained were those where people managed to take the land off of the real estate market through the use of community land trusts and low-income covenants in deeds. Market forces are extremely powerful and difficult to resist. The lesson I took away from my experience in Loisaida was the need to anticipate gentrification and secure control of the physical neighborhood as well as improve it. I reject the argument, however, that people should live in horrible circumstances to prevent gentrification. I believe that the type of occupation of neighborhoods I am advocating has the potential to both create alternatives *and* fight gentrification, but it requires solidarity, trust, time, and a lot of hard work.

All communities face specific challenges. Despite the relative poverty in Marshfield gentrification is not a big issue. We face very little development pressure and there is a good supply of low-income housing available. Nonetheless we have secured a degree of control over the physical environment of the town through the creation of community land trusts to insure an affordable housing stock that exists outside of the market, land trusts that conserve agricultural and forest land, town ownership of large conservation tracts, and progressive zoning developed by a volunteer board and voted on at town meetings. These are mechanisms available to both urban and rural communities. Obviously, these approaches do not constitute a revolution. They are tiny incremental steps that improve people's lives—they are just reforms. Do they buy into the system and support its continuation? They certainly can. But they may also constitute a first set of demands that can be continually expanded. If we have the vision of a free, just, and ecological society we must ask ourselves if these approaches take us closer to what we envision or move us farther away. I am not willing to wait for an insurrection before I engage in struggles that improve people's lives. I am not sure such a moment will come in my lifetime, and I reject the notion, bandied about in the 1960s, that the worse things get the more likely people are to revolt. In America, I fear, the worse things get the more likely people are to turn to forms of fascism. I think we need to dig-in, educate, organize, and develop relationships and counter-institutions that offer an alternative at the same time that we protest and oppose. I think it's possible to achieve reforms without becoming reformist. We need to keep our goal in mind, educate and take the incremental steps that can lead to real change. That's not as romantic as mounting the barricades, but it's the only way I know to bring about a new sensibility and transform the underlying structures that control our society.

Furthermore, I do not see the community-based approach I advocate as being the exclusive strategy to bring about the changes we so desperately need, but it is a *key* component that needs to be developed. I fail to see how we can possibly bring a decentralized, directly democratic society into being without a movement that creates direct democracy in our communities. Of course, we also need to continue to protest, both locally and nationally, and we also need to create other alternative institutions. The crises we face are so dire, compelling, and all-encompassing that there is need for work on all of these levels.

It is interesting to witness the more recent Occupy Our Homes and Occupy Sandy manifestations, which are important developments that begin to move in the direction I advocate. Engagement in struggles that have a direct impact on people's lives and communities help build relationships of trust and solidarity and reach people who would not become involved in oppositional "protest" politics. These relationships can provide a basis for further organizing, and an entry point for the creation of democratic forums at the neighborhood level that can serve to link issues of social inequity and a critique of capitalism and the larger social order directly to people's lives. Such forums can also be used to undermine the legitimacy of the centralized state and allow people to experience and imagine alternative ways of life.

Bringing Democracy Home

Actualizing these ideas will not be easy. It requires a commitment to becoming part of a physical community. It demands a recognition that change really does begin at home, and that the process requires grassroots-organizers ready to fight alongside their neighbors to bring a revitalized direct democracy to their communities. We must be prepared for a long-term struggle, and must ally ourselves actively with our neighbors. It is worth remembering that the Zapatistas spent more than ten years organizing in Tzotzil and other indigenous communities before they emerged to challenge the Mexican state.

In short, I believe that the concerns Occupy so effectively raised on Wall Street need to be brought home to our neighborhoods, and that the most effective way to do so is to establish real, face-to-face relationships in our communities and to raise these issues with our neighbors in the context of our shared lives. I do not believe that communities are the only place where struggle can occur. I recognize the catalytic role that the highly visible movement encampments played; I see the need for such manifestations, but I argue that they must now be linked directly to people's everyday lives. I recognize the importance—both symbolically and actually—of contestation at the points of power, like the Wall Street encampment, but I also recognize that participation in the actual encampment was largely limited to young people who had the ability to devote themselves to the project because they didn't have jobs, families dependent on them, or the other limiting factors that most people face. And even for these activists, the experience of the occupation was ephemeral, a "temporary autonomous zone" that was extremely important but ultimately unable to sustain itself. I would suggest that this is more often than not the case with movements that are purely oppositional or protest based. Occupy demonstrated that such movements are necessary but, in and of themselves, not in any way sufficient. I maintain that neighborhoods and communities are the most fruitful places to build democratic counter-institutions that can provide a basis for lasting change.

It would be foolish to believe that neighborhood assemblies and town meetings could supplant state power tomorrow. For one thing, many of our existing communities are mired in racism, classism, sexism, homophobia and all of the other ills of our existing society. We should use neighborhood forums as a vehicle for both education and action; a place to raise issues and discuss them with our neighbors. My experience has been that, when approached from this perspective, even very conservative neighbors have changed their views on critical issues like climate change, nuclear power, health care, and the banking system.

For this approach to successfully replace our current sham democracy a majority of the population must begin to practice direct democracy and they must do it where they live, revitalizing and reinventing our definitions of community and citizenship. Is it possible? Yes. Will it happen overnight? No. It is a massive educational project indeed, especially where there are reactionary attitudes that need to be overcome. But if we truly believe in democracy and empowerment this is just the work we need to do. It will not be easy, but without it I fear that we will continue to fall short of what it takes to transform the underlying structures of hierarchy and domination, and create a free society.

13968784R00106

Made in the USA
San Bernardino, CA
12 August 2014